Creating the New E-Business Company

Innovative Strategies for Real-World Applications

Michael P. Gendron

THOMSON

Australia · Brazil · Canada · Mexico · Singapore · Spain · United Kingdom · United States

**Creating the New E-Business Company:
Innovative Strategies for Real-World Applications**
Michael P. Gendron

Library of Congress
Cataloging in Publication
Number is available. See
page 218 for details.

For more information about
our products, contact us at:

Thomson Learning
Academic Resource
Center 1-800-423-0563

**Thomson Higher
Education**
5191 Natorp Boulevard
Mason, Ohio 45040
USA

CONTENTS

## CHAPTER 1

E-BUSINESS . . . NOT E-COMMERCE

E-Business . . . Not E-Commerce

E-business is a way of doing business that uses Web technology to improve your business. However, the tool will be effective only if people decide to do the right things, at the right time.

When people hear "e-business," they generally think selling over the Web—an easy misconception because the most easily observed applications are selling. The Web, however, is a tool that *accelerates communications* and allows for *instant transaction processing* and *elimination of manual, error-prone work*. The foundation of the "dot.com" era was built on the selling function using Web technology as the instant medium to complete the transaction. Entire companies with multibillion dollar market capitalizations were built on the future promise of sales to global markets, which were often multiples of existing markets and well outside the reach of many companies.

Companies were marketing products/services to individual consumers by "pushing"—bold banners, pop screens, banner-backgrounds for websites boasting of products and services, and intrusive mass e-mails promoting their wares. Companies focused on the technology and the potential sales markets and then urged consumers to buy products or services. Unfortunately, the Web is not a push technology, but a democracy. Pop-up banners, flashing backgrounds, and unsolicited e-mails can be easily ignored. Web advertisers have realized that "number of hits" or screen images do not convert to sales. Access to websites is virtually unlimited to anyone with access to the Web, but access is elective by the user. If users do not want to view an ad or e-mail, they ignore it or delete the mail. If consumers seek a product, service, or information, they can easily find it on the Web by using a well-developed browser.

The Web is an instant communication tool. Recall the afternoon that you wanted to plan your vacation to Park City, Utah. You entered "Park City" into your Yahoo!® search engine and instantly had a selection of Sponsor Matches offering ". . . Park City Hotels on Expedia . . ." ". . . Vacation Rentals . . ." and ". . . Park City & Dear Valley Reservations . . ." If you chose to search beyond the sponsors, you could either refine the search using the

"Advance Search" option, Ask Jeeves®, Google™, and so forth, or you could manually and slowly review several hundred thousand matches that included everything from the neighborhood florist, to local restaurants, to ski rentals. If you were in Paris, France, or Singapore when you had the urge to research the vacation opportunities, you would receive exactly the same information, instantly, regardless of your location. The question to be answered is, "How can you apply such versatility to your company?"

E-business and not e-commerce: Selling applies the Web business tool across functions, geography, and company lines to improve process. A company using *e-business* effectively will use the Web for communications (video, audio, print), research, transaction processing, and redesigning of processes and will use the Web wherever possible. In other words, *all functions must use the Web.*

This book will examine *e-business* by focusing on three axes of a well-managed business:

- *Functions* within a company (as defined by Michael Porter in his book *Creating and Sustaining Shareholder Value*) create value and do not just sell additional products to existing and new customers. A specific mix of functions, such as selling, distributing, manufacturing, marketing, and so on, make the company successful in a competitive market. As we apply "e-business" techniques to a company, we should select specific applications to beat competitors. For example, Amazon.com relies heavily on information technology (IT) and logistics to effectively serve the customer. Because they do not need manufacturing technology and research and development (R&D), their e-business application will focus on IT and logistics applications.
- *Activities* performed by functional organizations, such as communicating, research, and transaction processing, can easily be completed using the Web. In this book, we will review example functions within a company, discuss processes first to identify the activity needs, challenge the need for the activity, prioritize the activities based on importance to the firm, and then challenge you to use the Web to improve the value to the company.
- You must know the *constituents* that are affected by Web applications. Activities can affect the existing contacts (customers, vendors, employees, government agencies, communities, etc.), but they may also affect the global constituency—any people or organization anywhere on earth that have access to the Web. Companies should

think beyond current business to use the Web effectively. Have you used a Web browser to complete a search for something simple, such as a "Palm V," and instantly found a match with "Gray's Office Accoutrements" in London, England? As you apply Internet processes, *assume the world can see your work.*

Exhibit 1.1 depicts a simple returned goods transaction. Although initially you may expect that a returned goods authorization would affect the sales function and the customer, as you examine the returned goods process, you will see that the transaction affects additional functions and various "constituents" (both inside and outside the company), and it involves many activities, which are primarily transaction-oriented. Once you flowchart the transaction, you will see how an instant Web transaction can improve information flow, reduce errors, and ensure consistent clear communication among all the constituents. This book will help you prioritize the functions that would benefit from e-business and will also identify the constituents affected by e-business and the transactions that can be improved through enablement. This book will also help you implement changes in processes and culture to ensure that you gain the full benefit of *e-business.*

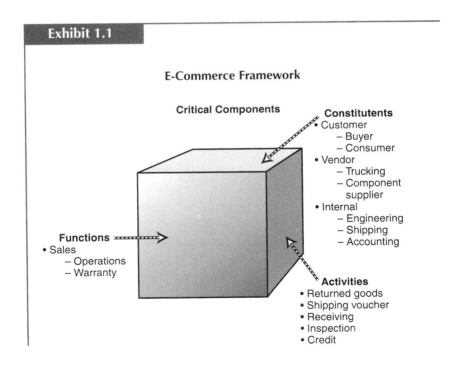

Exhibit 1.1

E-Commerce Framework

Critical Components

Constitutents
- Customer
  - Buyer
  - Consumer
- Vendor
  - Trucking
  - Component supplier
- Internal
  - Engineering
  - Shipping
  - Accounting

Functions
- Sales
  - Operations
  - Warranty

Activities
- Returned goods
- Shipping voucher
- Receiving
- Inspection
- Credit

The Web will stress executives as they confront the breadth and scope of the Web and its capabilities. The Web is global, instant, and transparent. Web team members need to work together to realize the full impact of the Web. This book will help Web executives expand their Web uses beyond the existing applications and challenge how each company operates.

Using the Web creates a faster pace within the company that is driven by the following:

- Multiple Web users, continually evaluating the applications and challenging the presentation and content of the company's site. Executives responsible for well-managed sites will encourage this interactive nature and will schedule site updating so that users will remain interested.
- Competitive websites that will accelerate the pace of your e-business applications because everyone—customers, competitors, vendors, and so forth—will compare competitive sites to yours.

E-business will make your business leaner, more efficient, and creative. Each of the activities—two-way communications, research, and transaction processing—performed in a "dot.com" company is valuable, but only if the activity has been well planned and properly justified for your business and effectively serves the constituents. Imagine the Human Resources (HR) department that loads images of insurance forms on a website (supposedly Web enabled) but does not make the forms interactive.

Value of E-Business

An effective e-business will be more profitable, have higher returns on equity and assets employed, require fewer employees per dollar of sales, and as a result, trade at a higher stock multiple. The improved metrics of an effective e-business will not necessarily result from employee terminations and the sale of assets but may result from broadly expanded markets and sales. Your company will be viewed as more progressive and willing to take calculated risks to improve the value of the company. Today, companies can change each of the activities (communications, research, and transaction processing) to improve their operations, earnings, and asset utilization.

In the past, many companies tried to justify Web programs by focusing on increased sales, but increased sales represent only a small benefit of Web enablement. If we assume that most activities in a company can be improved using the Web, this book will provide a framework to examine the functions, activities, and constituents for enablement. This book will demonstrate through examples how successful companies have improved earnings, return on investment, and overall company performance using the Web.

Review of a simple company with pretax profits of 10 percent of sales and a 10 percent return on equity will demonstrate how the market will value improvements in your operating ratios. A company's market valuation will be affected by how well you engage the Web and how advanced the investors consider a company to be.

If you think of a business as built on a foundation of interlocking blocks designed to provide a product to customers, each block is a functional area that contributes to the successful delivery of the product. The blocks may have a different number and type of people, different asset investments, and various communication patterns and activities. This book will help you systematically examine each of the building blocks within a company to identify the best Web applications and successfully implement the Web process.

Exhibit 1.2

Company = Organization of Functions

A company is built of many different functions, some of which are critical success factors in the industry. For example, in a high-tech industry, R&D and sales operations may be the critical functions to effectively serve the marketplace. In such a company, these functions represent a higher proportion of management attention and resource, as depicted in the illustration.

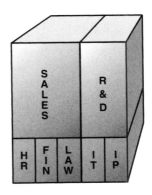

HR = Human resources
FIN = Finance
LAW = Legal and law
IT = Information technology

IP = Intellectual property
R&D = Research and development;
new product development

The following abbreviated financial statements will help us identify the Web impact on a business by understanding the constituents and how activities can be completed or perhaps eliminated using the Web. The opportunities identified have all actually been used in companies to improve performance, and they may be used in your company as well.

Brainstorming

	Baseline (Millions $)	Opportunities	Value	Potential
Sales	1,000	A, B, C	50	1,050
Gross Margin	500	D, E, F	40	540
Selling Expense	200	G, H, I	10	190
Marketing	100	J	5	95
Administrative	100	K, L	5	95
Total Expense	400		20	380
Pretax Earnings	100		60	160
Accounts Receivable	150	M	30	120
Inventory	125	N	40	85
Fixed Assets	300	O	50	250
Capital Employed	575		120	455
Return on Capital	17.4%		16.7%	35.2%

Studies show that approximately "60 percent of operating costs are personnel-related ...".[1] Let's examine some of the opportunities that may be available to *any* business, provided that they improve the process, the product, or service that the company now offers or may develop using the advantages of the Web. Our objective is to make the company more prosperous, not hi-tech. The examples represent minor improvements in expense investment, but combined with the improved sales and gross margin rate, they will result in a 60 percent increase in profitability. A company that embraces e-business will be creating a cultural revolution within the company and may be redefining the competitive framework in its industry; GE, Dell, and Amazon are excellent examples. These companies did not just make one-time improvements; they made cultural changes that require continued reinforcement. The process and product improvements will continue to generate improved value in a company.

The following note references (A, B, etc.) refer to the "brainstorming" financial statements presented previously.

A = New products, such as "information" about the business that can be sold to your customers. Product buying patterns, customer demographics, and

---

[1] Businessweek.com/ad sections; "Productivity and Performance: The Good News Gets Even Better," produced by The Custom Publishing Group, Cheryl Krivda. *Business Week*, 2003.

purchase timing may be valuable to vendors, but before the Web, the information could not be captured and communicated effectively. The use of bar codes at grocery stores makes it possible for merchants to provide "real-time" sales data to vendors, thereby improving the information they have about customers' purchasing habits and also eliminating steps and reducing costs in the reorder and restocking process.

B = Through "load management," airlines have identified ways to avoid empty seats on scheduled flights and to increase total revenue. Load management is a basis for joint marketing programs with resorts, rental car companies, local attractions, and so forth, which could never have been considered before real-time data. Real-time sales analysis can also be used to manage pricing and profitability for highly seasonal or limited life (e.g., fashion) merchandise by providing pricing incentives to buy before expiration. Real-time sales data have allowed companies such as the Gap to improve sales by redistributing merchandise among their stores as regional fashion trends are identified. Timely inventory movement reduces price discounting, space costs, obsolescence, and inventory investment, while serving the finicky customers more effectively. This would increase sales as well as reduce cost.

Load management is not just a tool used by the airlines. Pro sports teams have also started to use similar programs to improve sales and profits. "Eight teams, from baseball's Seattle Mariners to football's Green Bay Packers, are going online to do exactly what they long derided curbside scalpers for doing. They're directing hometown season-ticket holders to offer their unused seats on StubHub.com—and taking about a 10% cut when the tickets are sold. Eighteen other professional football, basketball, or hockey teams have put up their own sites to do much the same with the help of Ticketmaster. Pro basketball's Phoenix Suns are proving just how profitable the practice of home-team scalping can be: When the Cleveland Cavaliers' high-school phenomenon LeBron James came to Phoenix in November, the Suns' site got $300 for tickets that had a face value of $75."[2]

The key for these profit improvements is price-optimization (PO) technology, which is software that balances weighted variables such as current demand, inventory levels, desired sales velocity, profitability, and so forth. Many companies offer either stand-alone or fully integrated packages. Some companies that provide the software include i2 Technologies, Khimetrics, Metreo, ProfitLogic, Rapt, Vendave, and Zilliant. Company users extend from small local companies to some of the largest global companies, such as

---

2 "Don't Scalp Us. We'll Scalp You," by Brian Grow and Robert D. Hof, *Business Week,* April 19, 2004, p. 44.

Ford Motor Company, which uses PO technology to improve profits. As Lloyd Hansen, Ford's Vice President of Revenue Management, stated, "If better pricing tools and processes can improve revenue by just 1 percent, bottom-line profits would grow by 33 percent."[3]

C = Through careful buying pattern management, companies can recommend additional purchases to customers based on the buying patterns of others. Amazon.com uses this real-time marketing when a customer selects a particular book. Quite often, the system will automatically suggest, "Customers who bought this book also bought . . ." In the commercial environment, standard component packages could be offered during a purchase transaction. For example, when someone orders a laptop computer, which normally includes a standard carrying case, the software may also suggest an upgrade to a genuine leather case, perhaps some specific portable tools such as a back-up battery or a wireless modem. Based on the demographics, vendors may also use the data from your system to target promotions to specific customers. Is it likely that a company like Nordstrom could monitor buying patterns of crystal, for example, and notify you by e-mail that a sale is scheduled? In each case, the revenue value and customer profitability would increase with minimal incremental cost.

D, E, F = As each of these revenue examples increase, so would the gross margin. In some examples, there is little incremental cost (e.g., selling the demographic information to a vendor) and the gross margin would be 100 percent. Direct real-time linkages may also reduce the cost of doing business with your company and perhaps create a closer vendor/company relationship. Dell has created "real-time" linkages with critical vendors, thereby reducing transaction costs, errors, and inventory investments by moving to real-time processing. These linkages improve the partner relationship and improve overall profitability for both the vendors and Dell. Wal-Mart also uses information to improve service (the shelves are always properly replenished) and reduce operating costs, overstocks, and errors. Improved relationships may not be easily quantified but may be a significant competitive advantage. Some very progressive companies are using the Web to reduce shipping costs by purchasing "LTL" (less than truckload) space real-time on the Web. Wireless communications allow truckers to identify potential customers on the Web and fill their trucks on previously "deadhead," nonrevenue runs. Modern GPS (Global Positioning System) and wireless communications also allow for real-time equipment tracking,

---

[3] "The Right Price," by Russ Banham, *CFO Magazine*, October 2003, pp. 66–72.

reducing downtime and effectively increasing capacity with no incremental investment.

G = The information in your system can substitute for purchased market research, reducing your research cost, and internal sales statistics can improve your marketing dollar value by allowing better focus. If you can target a customer or group with a promotion, cost per promotion dollar will be less.

H = As you automate the selling function, you may find fewer errors in pricing, bidding, promotions, and so on. Automated processes will reduce clerical work and the number of errors and will improve the process cycle time.

- Real-time access to competitive product price, warranty, specifications, delivery availability, and so forth, obtained from the competitor's website can reduce research cost but may also provide information for higher selling prices.
- Progressive companies will have online templates of board of director's presentations and financial justification. Real-time access allows changes to the variables, such as project terms, interest rates, trade-in values, and so on, and preparation of an updated proposal immediately.

These presentations can be interactive and fully approved by home-office experts in proposal design, finance, and marketing to ensure that a well-developed, consistently prepared, debugged presentation is always up to date.

I, J, K, L = Overall administrative expense can be reduced by eliminating written reports (review time, printers, supplies, postage, and distribution costs). Also, many internal administrative activities (insurance registrations, intercompany charges, T&E, status reports, customer feedback, etc.) can use Web processing to reduce administration costs. In addition to these more mundane applications for the Web, think about the benefits of e-learning, which include better-trained personnel, improved customer service, and higher morale for those who take advantage of e-learning to further develop their careers. In June 2002, Grant Thornton, a global accounting firm with nearly 22,000 employees and almost $2 billion of revenue, created Grant Thornton University (GTU), "which is a single-entry point on the company's intranet for employees to access more than 1,000 hours of learning."[4]

Marketing expense can actually be an investment in an element of direct selling and new product development, using buyer intelligence to package or bundle products in the most desirable packages. "The next tool Ford

---

4 "Driving Performance: Human Capital," by Kara Parlin, *Internet World,* March 1, 2003.

is wielding is the Package Optimizer—a Web-based market-research tool marketed by Morepace International Inc. that packages the best mix of options to appeal to customers in a particular market. 'We've seen a lot of revenue improvement by selling features like DVD entertainment systems, heated and cooled seats, and navigation systems,' says Hansen (Ford's VP of Revenue Management) . . . 'We do an Internet survey of people in a simulated free-demand situation in which they are asked to build their ideal vehicles within the constraint of prices they can afford.'"[5]

M, N, O = In each of these balance sheet investments, speed and efficiency reduce the investment and improve productivity.

- M = A company's production cycle is reduced, and the products are shipped faster to improve their competitive position. Companies that can meet the ever-increasing demands of their customers can negotiate better sales terms, pricing, delivery, and so forth, with the customers. Better, quicker, cheaper is an excellent competitive weapon. If you don't fully engage in e-business first, will you trail the competition? Dell provides perhaps one of the best examples of benefitting from improved production cycle times. By using e-business concepts, Dell has less than 4 days' supply of inventory on hand, improved margins resulting from the sale of only the most advanced products, and lower receivables due to their build-to-order processing, which invoices the customer upon direct shipment.[6]
- N, O = Ford Motor Company also uses Web-based software to assist dealers in maintaining optimal inventory levels, which requires minimal working capital. "The last piece of the revenue-management strategy is currently being rolled out to dealers as Ford's Smart Order system, a Web-based tool that dealers can use to select the optimum inventory. 'Forty percent of inventory turns over in 30 days, while 45 percent sits there for more than 90 days,' says Hansen. 'By helping dealers figure out what to order based on profit margins, customer preferences, and the most appealing price, dealers can close sales much faster.' One dealer that has used the program has decreased his floor-planning cost by 25 to 30 percent."[7]

Better asset utilization will reduce capital investment and improve return on capital.

---

[5] "The Right Price," by Russ Banham, *CFO Magazine,* October 2003, pp. 66–72.

[6] "How Efficient Is That Company?" by Susan Scherreik, *Business Week,* December 23, 2002, pp. 94–96.

[7] "The Right Price," by Russ Banham, *CFO Magazine,* October 2003, pp. 66–72.

Company Will Be Worth More

These simple improvements are only a small selection of possible process improvements. Successful e-business companies empower their employees to identify, justify, and implement the improvement programs and invigorate the entire workforce—and not just the executives—to a more creative and productive state. Companies that have implemented e-business generally have higher stock market valuations, not just because of the improved financial results, but because they have demonstrated to the market that they are progressive and use modern management processes.

GE, often considered one of the best-managed companies in the world, has defined e-business as one of their strategic priorities during the next decade. They are one of the largest manufacturing companies in the world, with a record number of consecutive earnings growth by quarter, which enjoy a price earnings (PE) multiple more than double the PEs of their competitors. Amazon has a market capitalization of *$9 billion* and has *earned less than $10 million cumulatively* since its inception. These valuations may seem to represent a new financial theory, but in fact they represent the free-market's ongoing estimate of their future worth. These companies have embraced a new management philosophy—e-business—and have invested in infrastructure, hiring the right people to make their global business a success (see Exhibit 1.3).

This book will show you how to identify, prioritize, and implement Web opportunities in each functional area in your organization. Making your operation more enabled is not cost prohibitive, but it can be self-funding depending on your rate of change. You will also find that as you enable your operation, employee attitudes will improve and employees will become more productive and creative.

Summary

This book will assist you to:

- *Assess:* Assess processes, organization structure, and personnel to be certain that they are aligned with the company strategy.
- *Strategize:* Develop a strategy with performance goals and broad deliverables, once you understand the technical aspects and capabilities of e-business.
- *Prioritize:* E-business actions should be coordinated and prioritized as changes are implemented and the competition adapts to e-business. Prioritize some early wins and some self-funding projects to demonstrate results to employees, vendors, and customers.

Exhibit 1.3

Value to the Company

	Ratios			Competitive Information			Notes
	PE	Market Capitalization	Price to Book Value	PE	Market Capitalization	Price to Book Value	
General Electric	30	450 Billion	4	12	Up to 48 Billion	4	GE stock price has dropped by about 50 percent during the past few months. Historical ratios and not the most recent values used in the above summary.
eBay	87	23 Billion	6.4	30	8 Billion	4	
Amazon	&	9 Billion	&	33	8 Billion	4	Amazon has not had any appreciable earnings since its inception. Valuations based on typical ratios are meaningless—PE ratio is division by zero.

- *Realign:* Realign the organization structure, employees, and external resources to effectively "E-nergize" the company. This book will provide some practical guidelines to make these realignments quickly and effectively. Culture change will require the right people, in the right place, at the right time.
- *Execute:* Execution will be uneasy when you begin enablement because you will feel like you are giving up control. Enablement challenges the competency, flexibility, and stature of the business leaders, so be confident in your abilities, judgment, and leadership skills and enjoy the challenge.

CHAPTER 2

INTRODUCTION TO TECHNOLOGY

Introduction

E-business is built on a framework of information technology (IT) and is often explained with jargon, acronyms, and unfamiliar terms such as *spider, worm,* or *gopher* to describe Internet actions. Although it may sometimes be humorous to hear these terms, they are often misunderstood. As you discuss the Web with technical experts, have you stumbled through the conversations asking, "What is . . .

> . . . a **Wi-Fi?** . . . an *FTP?* . . . a **LAN?** . . . a **WAN?**
> . . . an **RBOC?** . . . *Vaporware?*" and so on.

Although the best IT executives and personnel try to translate these terms to those easily understood by non-IT personnel, the terminology is often very compact and, as a result, a very ineffective means to communicate outside the IT profession.

This chapter will review the World Wide Web (WWW), Web, or "Internet" terminology to acquaint you with the basics. Because the Web regenerates quickly, new terms are frequently developed, so be sure to expand your vocabulary of the basics by listening to the current experts. This chapter will describe the Web and Internet activities in unique terms. These terms appear in **bold italics** when first discussed, and at the end of the chapter, definitions of these terms will be included in alphabetical order.

Overview

Think of the Internet as a blend of hardware and software, similar to the existing global telephone systems. Hardware components include telephone handsets, speakerphones, modems, private branch exchange (PBX) stations, and the carrier's investment such as fixed-lines (fiber optic or copper cable), dish antennas and satellites, and signal-switching gear. Each component performs a unique function to ensure that data and voice reach the receiver at the correct destination, on time and complete. Global software standards and coding ensure that the signals travel throughout the networks to reach the correct destination.

The Internet is also a combination of hardware and software, developed to uniform, global standards to ensure that digital information is routed through the Web to its proper destination and then decoded so that the end-user receives useful information. The Internet transmits over the same phone medium as a telephone call. When you sit at your computer and generate a message to another person, the computer converts the message to digital format, creates a "to" and "from" digital address, breaks the message into uniform packets of data, and launches the data packets simultaneously through many different routes on the Internet, using local lines, high-speed transcontinental backbone lines, and routers, to be reassembled at the destination for viewing by the recipient. Let's review some of the major hardware and software elements used to achieve this:

- Hardware.
  - Global infrastructure. Hardware outside your four walls to make connections and transmit data.
  - Personal or company hardware. Hardware that you own or lease "within" the four walls to make connections and transmit data.

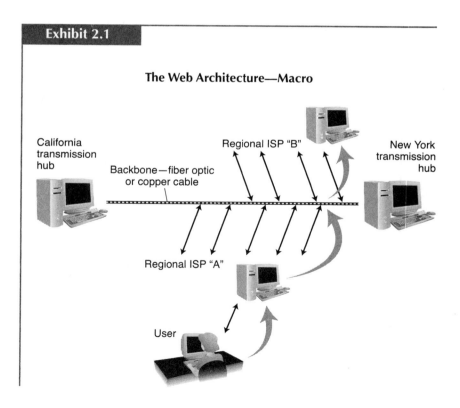

Exhibit 2.1

The Web Architecture—Macro

- Software.
  - Global, uniform software and software infrastructure to organize Web communications and also to provide a secure information environment.
  - Personal or company software used to make the Internet a more useful, productive, and secure business tool.
  - Content or file types. Web pages, e-mails, files of data, and so on, that you use in your business.

Hardware

Global Infrastructure

Hardware used in the Internet includes a *backbone,* which is a trunk line that links sites around the United States and around the globe; *regional or local networks;* and computer switches called *routers.* The hardware backbone is the *broadband* pipeline, or conduit, for all Internet transmissions and may be fixed, land-based lines—*fiber optic* or copper—or wireless through satellites or cell site connections. These are the same lines and satellites used for telephone calls. Transmission lines may be called Integrated Service Digital Network *(ISDN),* Digital Service Lines *(DSL),* *broadband,* or *T1/T3* lines. All these types of lines are basically telecom lines that transmit data signals that originate as phone calls or Internet activity. See Exhibit 2.2, for example.

Internet traffic originates with a user, is often processed by a regional *Internet Service Provider (ISP),* and if the destination is outside the region, is directed to the backbone for routing along this information highway. In Exhibit 2.1, the message can be followed from the user, to regional ISP "A," across the backbone, and finally to regional ISP "B." Information is parsed into data packets and sent through the system, directed by routers (high-speed electronic "switches" that read the Internet addresses, and using the *TCP/IP* protocols, route the data packets to their final destinations).

An unusual feature of the Internet is that every computer or *server* accessing the WWW is a part of the Web as a destination or organization address. The Internet exists only because of all of the participating computers and servers, which contain the information accessed by the Internet users. As more computers and servers are linked to the Internet, the actual "Web" expands. These user computers/servers are linked either directly to the Web or through ISPs. Consistent, standard, and universal software rules have been developed to ensure that information (e.g., data, pictures, audio, video) can be transferred anywhere at any time. The software rules are

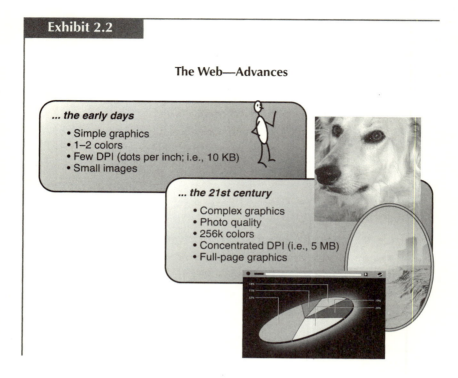

Exhibit 2.2

The Web—Advances

... the early days
- Simple graphics
- 1–2 colors
- Few DPI (dots per inch; i.e., 10 KB)
- Small images

... the 21st century
- Complex graphics
- Photo quality
- 256k colors
- Concentrated DPI (i.e., 5 MB)
- Full-page graphics

called *TCP/IP* (Transmission Control Protocol and the Internet Protocol) and provide the structure required to segment data into uniform transmission packets to be sent through the Web. Servers are separate computers whose sole purpose is to manage information, store *firmware,* and host home pages or websites. Servers accept communications from Web sources; check the information for such things as *viruses, worms,* or hacking (unauthorized use of your computer); complete the other assigned tasks, such as responding to questions (e.g., "Can you connect me to the online catalog that displays hiking equipment?"); provide answers to questions (e.g., FAQs, or Frequently Asked Questions); and store received and sent messages by server users.

Computers and servers are connected to the Web through the existing phone system, either through hard-wired lines or wireless connections. Hard-wired access may be through:

- *Direct connection—broadband:* Servers, local area networks *(LANs),* wide area networks *(WANs),* or large computers connect directly to the Internet, allowing direct high-speed access by any network users.

These high-speed connections often use broadband lines, such as T1 or T3 lines, or satellite downlinks.

- **Cable** *modem—broadband:* This device connects computers at speeds up to 100 times faster than an ordinary phone modem and provides two-way communication on the Web using TV cable installations.
- *ISDN and DSL—broadband:* These connections allow high-speed two-way communication through phone lines. ISDN requires a special ISDN modem and ISDN lines, whereas DSL uses regular phone lines (proximity to telecom infrastructure switching sites is required) and specially designed DSL modems.
- *Standard phone line ISPs and local phone services:* These services provide the slowest of hard-wired two-way communication and access to the Internet.

In addition to these hard-wired access types, wireless service may be available and includes the following:

- **Satellite** *access* (through the major satellite television services such as the Dish Network) offers high-speed downloading capability, with outbound communication through normal-speed telephone service.
- *Wireless service* (through digital cell phones or BlackBerry® devices) provides remote wireless access to the Web, wherever cellular signals are available, but it is relatively slow.
- *Wireless Fidelity* (Wi-Fi) services provide wireless connections to a local wireless hub. Wi-Fi service reception is localized within several hundred feet of the wireless hub. In early 2003, McDonald's restaurant and Starbucks introduced Wi-Fi to their customer experience. Hotels and airlines have also installed Wi-Fi for their customers, and sometimes the service is at no additional charge.

Although this is a brief summary of existing hardware, the capabilities of hardware and software that provide access to the Web improve almost daily. Many advances are covered in the press releases of high-tech companies as they introduce new products, but more often, you will become aware of advances by working with technical specialists. If you really want to keep up with the technology, keep in touch with the technical specialist.

Personal or Company Hardware

Certain access sites may actually be groups of computers or servers that are called WANs or LANs. WANs may span thousands of miles, whereas LANs may be within a building or office campus. The area network configuration allows for controlled access to specialty software, communications groups, and the WWW by individual users within the group.

WANs and LANs are often built around users with similar needs or who are in centralized locations or around those who may communicate frequently, such as customer service, finance, or perhaps research and development (R&D) engineering personnel. WANs link broader geographic users or possibly groups of LANs. General Motors may have a WAN in Detroit that links the finance LAN, manufacturing LAN, engineering LAN, and so on.

The WAN/LAN allows groups to communicate among themselves on their network and also provides access to the WWW. WANs and LANs are often created to manage information within a specific group with similar requirements. An engineering LAN may process information, such as computer-aided design/manufacturing (CAD/CAM), e-mail, *message boards* or chat boards, and instant messaging within the engineering

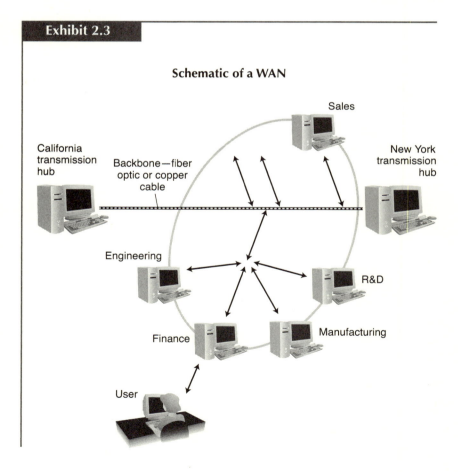

Exhibit 2.3

Schematic of a WAN

function. Software packages used exclusively by the engineering group may be accessible only to the engineers to improve security and reduce software costs that may be driven by the number of authorized software users.

LANs are not just limited to the business's or the organization's use because home users may also establish local networks, that is, using wireless-hub technology that accesses the Web through the hard-wired or wireless means described previously and then broadcasts the signal within a short range (e.g., within a household).

Software

When users access the Web, they generally do one of three things:

- *Research information* using the Web to explore individual websites such universities, companies, public databases, and so on; conduct searches using search engines; or learn through self-study or group interaction.
- *Communicate* with others on the Web—friends, unknown individuals, businesses, organizations, and governments, potentially located across the globe.
- *Transact business* using the Web to order products or services, execute purchases, transfer money, and so on.

These activities process information through the Web infrastructure and also through personal software that creates Web pages, communicates, browses, searches, and so on.

Software can be broken into two segments:

- *Infrastructure:* Infrastructure software directs the functions outside your computer, organization, or network. This includes the software required to direct the transmission and routing data across the Web and the structural software that makes the Web more useful, such as ISP network software (**newsgroups, chat,** and **instant messaging**), **Internet telephony,** Web pages, **markup languages** (e.g., **XTML, XML, DHTML**), and **search engines** (which are sometimes called **Web crawlers** or **spiders**). Web structure segments users by major type into **domains,** such as government, .gov; organization, .org; or commercial, .com. Although the Internet is free and without major constraint, administrative organizations have created rules and standards to manage the information flow. Some of the key standard setters or Internet administrators are as follows:
  - **Registrars**
  - Internet Security Systems

- InterNIC
- ISP
- Servers
- Regional networks

- *Content and user software:* Personal software usually includes at least a Web browser (e.g., Microsoft Internet Explorer® or Netscape®) and may also include advanced software for Web page development, firewalls, antivirus programs, or audio/video software (e.g., *RealPlayer*® or Windows Media® player). Content may include data, images, messages, and standard features such as websites, Web pages, and software designed to make the Web a useful tool for communication, transaction processing, and research.

Infrastructure

As a user, when you access the Web, you are using either an ISP log-on and a default Web page provided by the ISP or a Web server *portal* such as Yahoo! All the "back room" tasks, such as page layout, typefaces, site address, and so on, are coded into the home page. Because Web infrastructure software is improving every day to increase efficiency and quality, we cannot discuss all the types of software and improvements in a book that is published on an annual cycle. Talk to your IT experts to keep up with the basics. Also, software that is used to actually encode and decode the digital signals and route them around the WWW, as well as software code used in the hardware itself, is outside the scope of general executive knowledge and will not be discussed in this book. However, we will explore some of the basic kinds of software present in the WWW. Web portals often provide access to many infrastructure software products. Progressive portals provide access to value-added services such as newsgroups, chat, and instant messaging services, and they may also have home page access to Web crawlers or spiders. The following products make the Web much more useful:

- *Newsgroups* are regulated or unregulated posting boards that are grouped by main topics, subtopics, and individual messages. Some messages are interconnected by threads, that is, linkages that provide a basic comment and all other comments that are meant to be associated with the initial comment. Regulated newsgroups are monitored by a site sponsor, which ensures that the comments relate to that particular newsgroup. Newsgroups are sometimes referred to as chat or message boards because they offer a public "posting" of information.

- *Instant messaging* is the result of advanced technology available on the Web. Major ISPs such as America OnLine (AOL®) and MSN® have developed software that allows online users to "talk" in real time. Specific users in the "group" of instant messengers can have an online dialogue when the users are live.
- *Search engines* (a.k.a. Web crawlers, spiders, etc.) are often a key element of the ISP home page. This infrastructure software allows a user to search the entire global Web for information specified in the search criteria. There are various levels of search engines, which can include basic engines, such as Google, AltaVista™, Hotbot™, or Lycos™, and higher-level, or meta, search engines that analyze data summarized in the basic search engines. Meta search engines search the databases established in the basic search engine databases.
- *Blogs* are uncensored, publicly accessible personal Web logs or journals that are updated daily. These are often searchable by search engines.

Each Web address has a unique **URL** (Uniform Resource Locator) that is similar to a business address at your company. The URL allows Web surfers to locate your business or Web page. Client and server software uses **HTTP** (Hypertext Transfer Protocol) or **HTML (Hypertext Markup Language)** to communicate. This "HTTP language" is a high-order language that allows print enhancements (bold, italics, and underlining) and improved formats.

Personal or Company Owned

Many types of software are broadly distributed and are often used by the average Web user. Web browsers are "client software"; that is, the computer operator owns or has the right to use the software on his or her computer, which allows the user to access the URL at the server address. Other types of personal software that you may acquire include firewalls, antivirus software, Adobe Acrobat®, SpamKiller®, RealPlayer, Internet Security, and so forth. To become familiar with the various types of software, I suggest that you browse the software section of Amazon.com; they have one of the most complete software selections available.

The **home page** is the primary access point to the URL and can be the index or table of contents of a few or hundreds of linked pages. A well-designed home page will include **hyperlink** text that, when double-clicked with a computer mouse, will automatically move the reader to the specific page referenced. A home page can include text, images, or hyperlinks to other completely independent sites—sites outside that particular URL.

Websites are often designed in a "tree" configuration that makes navigation easier by progressing through a well-defined series of activities to a final destination. Some websites may be designed just like a book—from front to back—without any design branches to follow, whereas others may be completely random, providing little guidance to the user. The best websites are user friendly and designed in the "tree" configuration. Let's look at an example of a "tree" configuration designed by Blister's Outfitters to guide a customer to their desired product, hopefully to be purchased.

Exhibit 2.4

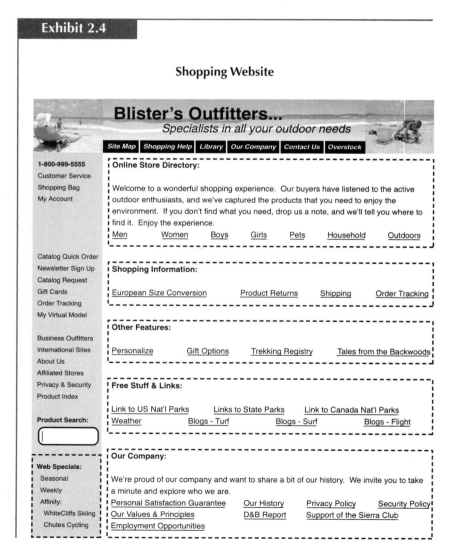

Shopping Website

Blister's Outfitters...
Specialists in all your outdoor needs

Site Map | Shopping Help | Library | Our Company | Contact Us | Overstock

1-800-999-5555
Customer Service
Shopping Bag
My Account

Online Store Directory:

Welcome to a wonderful shopping experience. Our buyers have listened to the active outdoor enthusiasts, and we've captured the products that you need to enjoy the environment. If you don't find what you need, drop us a note, and we'll tell you where to find it. Enjoy the experience.

Men   Women   Boys   Girls   Pets   Household   Outdoors

Catalog Quick Order
Newsletter Sign Up
Catalog Request
Gift Cards
Order Tracking
My Virtual Model

Shopping Information:

European Size Conversion   Product Returns   Shipping   Order Tracking

Business Outfitters
International Sites
About Us
Affiliated Stores
Privacy & Security
Product Index

Other Features:

Personalize   Gift Options   Trekking Registry   Tales from the Backwoods

Product Search:

Free Stuff & Links:

Link to US Nat'l Parks   Links to State Parks   Link to Canada Nat'l Parks
Weather   Blogs - Turf   Blogs - Surf   Blogs - Flight

Web Specials:
Seasonal
Weekly
Affinity:
  WhiteCliffs Skiing
  Chutes Cycling

Our Company:

We're proud of our company and want to share a bit of our history. We invite you to take a minute and explore who we are.

Personal Satisfaction Guarantee   Our History   Privacy Policy   Security Policy
Our Values & Principles   D&B Report   Support of the Sierra Club
Employment Opportunities

The architecture includes various groups of products and activities, which are really branches of decisions that can be made by the shopper. This kind of organization makes the Web search and purchase process easier to navigate. Good Web designers analyze how individuals access and use the website—in this case, for shopping—and design the site to provide the quickest, easiest, and most logical process for the customer to complete the desired transaction. Think about a website that you use frequently and recall the information groupings that effortlessly take you through to your destination.

The WWW's value is based on the vast amount of information immediately accessible to any user. However, with millions of terabytes of information, it would be impossible to use the Web effectively without some kind of master Web design or strategy, such as search engines. Web users will find that **Internet search engines** (e.g., Google, Lycos, Excite®) are invaluable research tools. The engines are large databases that are frequently updated using Web crawlers or spiders. Users access the databases to locate other websites or specific information on the Web. As the name implies, the Web crawlers or spiders roam the Internet to identify and assemble information from the Web into logical databases. The information is indexed or categorized based on key words in the websites. As a user searches—or surfs—the Web for information, words or phrases are matched with those in the indices and summarized in a list of sites accessible with a double-click on the hotlink.

Meta search software is a more advanced search engine that runs multiple searches through many existing databases to simplify the search process. Intelliseek uses meta search software called BullsEye®, whereas Copernic is an independent, separate search agent that polls many different search engines. The advantages of these meta search software packages is that all of them can search and analyze search engine databases—up to 1,000 separate engines—simultaneously, summarize search results, monitor changes to sites, and actually report activity through periodic e-mails. As results are reported to the user, premium meta search software may also prepare a brief summary of information contained in the referenced URL, which, of course, is immediately accessible with a quick double-click of the mouse on the **hotlink.**

In addition to the search applications, users may send information using **POP3** with attachments—such as Microsoft Word® or Excel® documents, **JPEG** images, **streaming video, streaming audio,** music files such as **MP3** and **video conferencing**—over the Web. The video/audio files create images or sounds for the user that were recorded/observed using electronic devices, translated into digital code, condensed using mathematical algorithms, and transmitted for retrieval by a software request. "Streaming" is just as it sounds—displaying stored or live action sights and sounds, such as from a video camera or audio recorder to your computer.

Another feature of the Web that frightens many of the long-distance carriers is **voice-over IP.** Because information transmitted over the Web is always a digital transmission, it is possible to communicate with other Web users by using software in each computer that converts data packets into sound—hence, voice over the Web using IP (Internet Protocol). Voice-over IP allows for voice transmission from one computer to another through the Web, without regard to the distance. If a Web user wants to "talk" through the Web, the user only needs to have the software at each computer to communicate. Because many Web ISPs have a single charge for unlimited use, it is possible to speak on a long-distance "call" for an unlimited time without any additional charge. How many of your business associates have used this feature to call home—in Italy, Germany, China, India, and so on? Think about a 2-hour call to India, at no charge. Some companies have taken advantage of the IP technology and established new businesses using voice-over IP. The "10-10-220" phone system uses the technology to avoid long-distance charges while providing point-to-point service.

A major customer service outsourcing organization assessed their service needs and discovered three essential elements to the service: English speaking, 7/24 hour service, and technically savvy customer service personnel. They also reviewed available resources in the United States and discovered that qualified personnel to "man" the phones would cost, including salary, fringe benefits, vacations, and so on, about $30 per hour. As they evaluated the potential solutions, they considered establishing the outsource service in India, the Philippines, and Ireland. The maximum out-of-pocket cost per hour in each location varied from $10 to $13 per hour. Long-distance phone charges were a major obstacle for such a service. After a thorough investigation of international rates, long-term commitments, and voice-over IP, the company invested in its own server and hired the qualified workforce in India and Ireland. This provided global coverage, within a normal 12-hour workday, without premium 3rd shift time, and also provided flexibility around major government and religious holidays. Despite the incremental costs for the hardware, software, and separate centers required in both Ireland and India, cost savings totaled millions of dollars per year.

One of the programming languages that you often hear of is *Java,* which is a powerful programming code that can be used on many different types of computers, simply by "compiling" the language on that particular computer. Typically, programs that are written for a Macintosh (Mac) will not work on a Windows-based machine (a so-called PC machine). Java eliminates that problem and allows for Web simplification for Mac users. Software code in Java can be used in PCs, Macs, and even some personal digital assistants (PDAs), such as Palm™ devices. Once again, universal standards allow for dramatic improvements in effectiveness.

Have you heard of Napster™? Napster is the file-downloading website that was notorious for allowing the free download of prerecorded copyrighted music and videos. In 2003 the U.S. courts restricted some of Napster's copy features, but at the same time, other free services have started. There are many similar alternatives available.

File downloads often require a long time when using phone modem Web access. For example, transferring a 5 MB file (5,000,000 bytes of information) at 56 KB/sec (kilobytes per second) will require about 1.5 minutes, if all goes through the Web as scheduled. As a way to reduce the file transfer time, files are compressed using specially developed standardized compression software— ZIP files in the PC environment or stuffed files for Macs. This refers to file compression software such as PKZip™, WinZip®, SimplyZip™, or other packages used extensively for Web applications, which have basic versions that are free and are easily downloaded from the Web. Compression software reduces file sizes anywhere from 90 percent for Word documents to as little as 10 percent for detailed graphics or pictures. Think about that 1.5 MB file— rather than 1.5 minutes for transfer, wouldn't 10 seconds be better? Compression is the foundation of *multicast IP* broadcasts, which are built on compressed audio and video files.

Audio files are now available in several formats that can be played using software or devices such as RealPlayer or Windows Media player, MP3, or most recently iPod® from Apple. All these formats provide the same basic product—digital audio that may be stored on your computer hard drive, CD-ROMs, or MP3 or iPod players. Most recently, Steve Jobs and Apple Computer have used the Web to change the music industry. In 2002 and 2003, Steve Jobs worked with the recording industry and artists to develop a new format and process to distribute music. In May 2003, Apple Computer, in cooperation with several major media companies, announced that they would offer individual songs over the Internet, providing unlimited use, for only $0.99 per download. This is the first time such a low-cost concept has actually been implemented. For only $0.99, the user receives a playable song, and with virtually no incremental cost, the recording and media companies have nearly $0.99 of incremental earnings. The concept eliminates the music retailer and still provides a reasonable margin for the media company and the artist. When you consider that individual songs can be purchased for $0.99, how much different is that than buying a $12 CD that includes 12 songs? However, in the CD sale, you have costs and profit sharing at the retailer and distributor, as well as CD production and packaging costs by the media company and shipping and handling costs. The Web is changing the business landscape.

Protection Software

Easy, global real-time access is the foundation of the success of the Web, but it is also a curse to be managed because file sharing and transfers expose your system to infection and hacking. Web viruses, worms, or other contaminants may infiltrate your computer system once you have opened your computer to the Web. You may also have to suffer with *spam* (junk e-mail), which can effectively disable your system by overwhelming the inbound mail channel. Profit-oriented entrepreneurs have also identified these Web failings and developed *firewalls, antivirus,* and other security and nuisance avoidance software. And with the Web being open to all people—including those creative and devious hackers, spammers, and Internet fraud purveyors—the developers of these safeguarding software programs have an unlimited supply of opportunities to sell you protection. Generally the protection programs are purchased software packages that also include free software updates for a specified period, for example, 1 year. Software titles from companies such as Norton, McAfee, and Symantec do an excellent job for most users, both individual and corporate. Another form of WWW protection is *encryption* software, often provided through secure websites.

One feature of websites that is both helpful and potentially harmful is the *cookies* that are left on your computer when you access some Web pages. Cookies are personalized pieces of information deposited by websites on your computer. They are designed to improve the website's access by storing identifying information linked to your user address. The downside of a cookie is that personal information, such as the number, duration, and time of log-on, may be monitored by the website. However, you can manage your exposure by "blocking" these cookies from being left on your computer. This can be done by selecting the appropriate settings in your browser or through a separate utility program.

Audio/Visual Applications

The Web provides an inexpensive alternative for any distance communication process—audio, visual, or simply data. Innovative companies are now using Webcast software products provided by companies such as ATT, WebEx, and callrci.com. These conference products allow over-the-Web communications and can include file sharing, presentations, and live or streaming video. These products can be used for live two-way conferencing or for offline training.

Definitions

- *Antivirus:* Antivirus software was developed to stop viruses from attacking data systems on a computer. Antivirus software can block virus programs from entering your systems, notify the user of an impending virus attack, or eradicate infected programs from a system.
- *ASPs (application service provider):* Added–value service providers are private companies that provide software applications and storage for a fee (sometimes based on usage) to meet the users' requirements with little or no capital outlay. For example, global customer resource management (CRM) is available through http://www.salesforce.com to companies that need customer management with no initial capital outlay. Tour http://www.salesforce.com for a good example of a fully functioned ASP to manage customer resources.
- *Backbone:* Companies such as MCI (formerly named WorldCom Inc.) and Qwest built high–capacity or broadband U.S. and global transmission lines to carry the Internet traffic. These transmission lines could be fiber optic or copper cable, and they cross continents and oceans to link major regional networks. These are the primary transmission "pipes" that carry Internet traffic between major centers for final distribution to regional and local networks, and ultimately to an individual user. Backbones operate at more than 2.4 GB/sec (gigabytes per second). As of early 2003, the global backbone was operating at a very low percentage of capacity.
- *Broadband:* Broadband refers to a high-capacity line, or a line with "band width," which is important as the volume of data increases.
- *Chat:* A real-time method of communicating with others on the Web using the keyboard to type messages in common areas or chat boards. Communications can be with one or many participants.
- *Cookies:* Pieces of data deposited on your computer to assist website servers in identifying the site user. Cookies are often used to track user activity and expedite access to specific sites such as Amazon.com.

- **Domains:** The domain process is a method to organize the Web more effectively into meaningful groups of users. There are more than 60 million Web users around the globe, each with a unique numerical identifier or address. Rather than have software search all 60 million individual names to efficiently sort to the final Internet address, users have been organized into domain subsections to allow for quicker, more efficient routing to the correct Web address. Some of the more common domains include ".com"—commercial, ".gov"—government, ".edu"—educational, or ".mil"—military. Private companies called *registrars* manage the domains.
- **Encryption:** Software that alters information using complex mathematical algorithms or formulas to ensure that the information cannot be intercepted and used by unauthorized personnel.
- **Firewalls:** Firewall software allows outward access to the Internet but controls external Internet users access to your system.
- **Firmware:** Firmware software is embedded in hardware, such as PCs, servers, or computer systems; is either fixed or upgradeable; and is used to make the hardware operate as designed.
- **FTP:** FTP stands for File Transfer Protocol. This is a standardized process that allows users to send files over the Web to other users; it also allows users to access files and download files from other websites.
- **Home page:** A website is often a collection or a group of pages maintained by that particular website. The home page is the top or first page in a website and generally includes an index to features within the site.
- **HTTP:** Hypertext Transfer Protocol language defines how the Web server and the Web browser interact.
- **Hyperlink or hotlink:** These are underlined or highlighted words or icons embedded in a Web page that will connect the user to other Web pages or sites when activated (i.e., when clicked).
- **Hypertext Markup Language (HTML):** HTML is a high-end software tool used to develop Web pages; it consists of commands that instruct the browser on how to display pictures, text, and cross-references to other Web pages and websites.
- **Instant messaging:** This software allows for real-time, immediate communications between individuals or groups using the Web.
- **Internet search engines:** This software routinely scans millions of Web pages, collects information from the pages (using Web crawlers or

spiders), and categorizes and stores the information in databases accessible by Web users.

- *Internet Service Providers (ISPs):* These organizations generally provide access to the Internet on a monthly subscription basis. Often, the ISPs provide toll-free connections to the Web through agreements with various local and long-distance telephone providers, regardless of your current location. For example, EarthLink® and AOL provide toll-free Web access virtually anywhere on the globe. When you sign on, the service immediately launches your personal home page, e-mail, predefined chat boards, and so on. Sometimes, the ISPs include additional value-added services (e.g., instant messaging, spam control, preferential shopping, parental controls, security for children) to maintain their competitiveness and market share. An excellent example of a "value-added" ISP is AOL, which continually upgrades the product offering and is accessible globally on a real-time basis.

- *Internet telephony; voice-over IP:* This type of software and hardware digitizes sound, compresses the code, creates unique data packets, and transmits the packets over the Web to others using software and hardware to convert the digitized code back to sound.

- *Java:* Java is a computer language that works on different kinds of computers, such as a PC (Windows-based computer), Macintosh, or UNIX-based system; it allows computers to interact with the Web and actually run programs through the Web browser.

- *JPEG:* Joint Photographic Experts Group developed a standard for graphics used on the Web. Photographs, charts, graphs, and cartoons can be developed in this file type, the file name of which ends with the extension ".jpeg". Files with the ".jpeg" notation can be read by standard software provided in basic browsers, such as Microsoft Internet Explorer, Netscape, WebView™, and so forth.

- *LAN:* A local area network is a group of computers/servers linked together by high-speed lines to improve security and access speed.

- *Markup languages:* These are software languages that provide instructions to the Web browser about how Web pages should look and sound and how to interact and link with other URLs.

- *Message boards:* These sites provide a public electronic posting medium about specific topics, ranging from companies, to diseases, to government policy, to virtually any topic imaginable. Because the Web is open to all people—worldwide—without any qualifying criteria, message boards may often include misinformation. When reviewing information posted on "boards," it is important to consider the qualifications of the source before you use the information for any significant decision. Sometimes limited-access message boards are used to manage major projects. Message boards are an ideal forum to share and discuss information that can help solve problems, when the problem solvers are scattered across a broad geography. R&D departments, product design departments, and sales organizations may save time and out-of-pocket costs by using message boards for collaborative developments and information sharing.

- *Meta search:* A meta search is similar to a search engine except that meta search combs the search engine databases for the characteristics being sought (i.e., it searches the search engines).
- *MP3:* MP3 is a music file format that has a quality equal to that of CDs. MP3 file sizes are much smaller than those of ordinary sound files.
- *Multicast IP:* This allows for video and audio broadcasts to occur with less consumed bandwidth than other protocols.
- *Newsgroup:* A newsgroup is a discussion forum on the Web on which notes about various topics are written, coordinated, and accessible through Usenet. Postings/news items are grouped by major subject categories, including news, rec (recreation), soc (society), sci (science), comp (computers), and so forth.
- *POP3:* This is an acronym for Post Office 3 communications protocol used to serve e-mail requirements. It is one of the most commonly used, and therefore universally acceptable, forms of e-mail transmission. Another similar protocol is SMTP, which stands for Simple Mail Transfer Protocol.
- *Portals:* Web users often use Web portals as the base for all their activity. Portals, such as Yahoo!, MSN, or AltaVista, are "home bases" that can be customized to present frequently viewed information as the main page. Specific information, such as current news, sports, stock quotes, company information, and weather, can be predefined.
- *RealPlayer:* RealPlayer is a software product produced by RealNet that makes it possible to play video and/or audio through your computer. Files played can be either imported and saved for later viewing/playing or played "live" as streaming video/audio directly from a website.
- *Regional or local networks:* These are smaller "pipes," or transmission lines, that access and transmit Internet data from the backbone and

then route information to the ultimate users. RBOCS (Regional Bell Operating Companies) or other intermediaries called *ISPs* often manage these networks to traverse the "last mile" to the users.

- *Registrars:* Registrars are private companies that help manage the Web environment by managing the many domains on the Internet, such as *.com, .gov,* and *.org.*
- *Routers:* Routers are Web infrastructure hardware components that are located throughout the Web to direct, or "route," the data to a predefined address in the most effective way. Data (pictures, voice, scripts of words, or numbers) are digitally encoded, parsed into uniform sized packets, and transmitted throughout the Web so that all data packets are assembled at the destination in their complete form, to be interpreted by the user's computer.
- *Search engines:* A search engine is a database of information, frequently updated by Web crawlers or spiders, that examines and categorizes information contained on millions of Web pages.
- *Servers:* Servers are computers that perform tasks as directed by other computers. Servers may store Web pages or data accessible through the Web and also may send and receive e-mails, monitor Web activity, and control communications and content (e.g., pornographic controls, spam, firewalls for security, antivirus software).
- *Spam:* Spam is the equivalent of junk mail—unsolicited commercial advertisements or communications distributed over the Web to addresses from mailing lists purchased or compiled from organizations.
- *Spider:* Spider software searches the Web and assembles an array of information into a searchable database, which is then accessible by search engines.
- *Streaming audio:* Streaming audio software allows users to listen to sounds and/or music on their computers as the file is being transferred to their systems.
- *Streaming video:* Streaming video software allows users to view videos on their computers as the file is being transferred to their systems.
- *TCP/IP (Transmission Control Protocol/Internet Protocol):* The IP is the addressing system that allows data to be routed throughout the system. Addresses are numerical codes or addresses like street addresses or phone numbers that are unique to each user. The TCP is the rule that segments the information into uniform data packets that traverse the Internet. Data packets may not travel in the same path because it may not be the most effective method to route the data to the

destination, but will be routed through the Web to be viewed at the destination as a single image. Routers perform this transmission task.

- *Transmission media.* These include the following:
  - *Cable and satellite:* TV cable lines are used in home and business installations for Web access. The most visible company providing this service in the United States is AOL/Time Warner. Satellite TV providers, such as the Dish Network, also provide broadband Web access for downloading.
  - *DSL:* Digital Service Lines (DSL) use existing telecom lines, are used for high-speed local access to the Web, and require a special DSL modem for access. DSL access must be close to phone company substations due to technical constraints and therefore may not be available in all locations. DSL lines are very popular because they are relatively inexpensive, easy to set up, and provide high data transmission rates at reasonable cost.
  - *Fiber optic:* Broadband optical fiber lines are generally used for long-distance (transoceanic or transcontinental) data transmission. Recently, fiber-optic lines have also been installed in LANs, WANs, and regional markets for high-volume broadband transmissions.
  - *ISDN:* Integrated Service Digital Network (ISDN) uses existing phone lines and is generally used for high-speed or broadband local access to the Web. ISDN requires special modems. Transmission rates can range up to 129 KB/sec.
  - *T1 and T3 lines:* These are the highest-speed local access lines used by individuals or companies. These lines are generally rented or leased as dedicated lines on a long-term basis, have a higher fixed cost than DSL or ISDN lines, and require specialized equipment to operate. Costs could exceed $800 per month. Transmission rates range from about 1.5 Mbps (megabits per second) for a T1 line to 44.8 Mbps for a T3 line.
- *URL:* The Uniform Resource Locator is similar to a post office or mailing address specifically used on the World Wide Web. The URL indicates the host computer location, website, name of the Web page, and type of file.
- *Vaporware:* In the "dot.com" heyday, software and Web companies popped up like weeds in a fertile field, often making extraordinary promises for speed or performance software or websites that were beyond the imagination and the delivery. Often, these promised

results were, at best, wishful thinking, but they were quite often "vaporware"—something that did not or could not exist as committed.

- *Video conferencing:* This software allows live interaction video/audio with other users through the Internet.

- *Viruses:* Viruses are harmful programs that infiltrate your data system by attaching themselves to programs and/or files that you download. Viruses are disruptive, and sometimes extremely harmful, to your data files, executable files, file directories, or basic system files.

- *WAN:* A wide area network is an organization of local area networks (LANs) connected by high-speed data systems (phone lines, wireless, cable, and so forth) to provide rapid and secure service to defined users.

- *Web crawlers:* This type of software searches the Internet, identifying and capturing data that can be used for categorizing information in databases used by search engines.

- *Worms:* A worm is a computer program, similar to a virus, that replicates itself, resides in an operating system, and is an executable program that can delete files or send e-mails.

- *XTML; XML; DHTML:* Each of these acronyms represents a "markup language," which computer programmers use to develop Web pages. Programmers use these languages to write programs that make Web communication simpler and to create richer text and graphics. Depending on the markup language selected, the language allows developers to communicate with many electronic devices (e.g., handheld computers, handheld devices, cell phones) or to communicate dynamically (e.g., to create "moving pictures" on a website).

Summary

By now, you have a brief idea of Web structure and terminology, and you can understand that the Internet has created a totally new business environment for activities such as communication, transaction processing, and research. Real-time global activity is available today, if you have the drive. Unfortunately, the WWW pace changes terms and available features frequently. It is not essential that an executive keep current on all terms, but you should keep up to date on major changes. Make it your organization's responsibility to monitor changes in terminology and technical innovations and to keep you informed. In the next chapter, we will discuss various analytical approaches to using these technologies to make the company better.

## Chapter 3

Framework for Developing E-Business Strategy

Introduction

As we speculate about how we can improve our business operation, two entrenched camps form about Web enablement and e-business focus:

NO!

"It's **too complicated** to do effectively. The process we use now—although not perfect—will get us through. We should wait until more resources are available to do it right and just **patch up** the existing process."

"It will **cost too much** to implement, and I'm not sure that we can justify it."

YES!

"Let's get this thing implemented—perhaps a **pilot project to start**—but let's start the process to see if the premise makes sense."

Often, as we consider ways to improve the business, we default to cost-cutting measures as the best, least risky, and quickest solution. Think about the number of one-time charges—no matter how repetitive—reflecting a restructuring that you have seen during the past 6 months. As an alternative, we should focus on profits and value creation, which may include cost cutting—selectively, not across the board—and also investing in specific functions and activities—again, selectively, not across the board. As "C" level executives, we often discuss our businesses as the company, expenses, head count, assets, customers, and so on. In this chapter we will explore a process to identify the critical components of our business by understanding the value-added activities and investment areas, the impact on the constituents, and how we can use the Web to improve the business.

The approach is based on the new global competitive environment for our products and the impact on our constituents since the explosion of Internet usage. Today, because innovation and change are so rapid and the constituents are now global and beyond our typical business horizon, we cannot review the business as in the past. We will examine our business to identify changes in investment, activities, and cycle time using the Web in this new environment.

Broad Picture

Just as in any "lean" business, if we improve only a few pieces of the business without understanding the total impact, we may actually destroy value by adding costs to total. For example, companies sometimes focus only on the component "purchase price" as a measure of success. But will a 20 percent component cost saving by sourcing that precisely engineered component from China actually increase total company cost? Possibly yes, because occasionally a Chinese translator may be required—on short notice and at high cost—because the shipment of critical parts is 3 days late . . . and we shut down the production line . . . and no one in the Shanghai shipping department speaks English . . . and airfreight is required (at 25 times the normal cost) because the normal ocean shipping lead time is 6 weeks (and, oh by the way, normal ocean shipping costs 3 times the cost of domestic freight cost) . . . and did we mention that a 3 month's supply of inventory generally must be kept on hand, just in case there is some kind of glitch . . . and the inventory required rework, but we could not afford to return the product to China . . . and so forth . . . and the cost of sending our engineers to China on a 2-week trip is $25,000. . . .

Instead, let's examine our business as a whole by examining the primary processes embedded in the value chain of the company, which will be explored at length in Chapter 4. We will examine the quantity and type of resources required to operate the company, process cycle time, and the amount of actual activity to complete the value chain. You will not be surprised to find that much of your cost and added value is driven by people, processes, and interaction among various constituents inside and outside the company.

As we examine the value chain, whenever possible we will eliminate non–value-added tasks, reduce activity time, and minimize investments in people and assets, ideally to be redeployed to value-added alternatives. We will use the Web as a process improvement tool for *communications, research,* or *transaction processing,* and we will change the pace of our business to meet the global market needs. One key to "E" success is to think "F-A-S-T." The pace of our business must be tuned to the marketplace—the constituents, customers, vendors, employees, governments, and even the competitors—and not to our internal company routine. Under the old paradigm, we were allowed months to execute without stress or penalty; today, we may have days or hours to respond to the global marketplace.

We will start by summarizing the business using published financial information, recast considering the types and quantity of resources used, functions within the value chain, and the benefits of each investment. As an example, Exhibit 3.1 depicts the costs in a profit and loss (P&L) statement in three main groups:

- Personnel cash expenditures
- Nonpersonnel cash expenditures
- Noncash expenditures

In the example, a large portion of cost is people, including outside consultants. People perform activities in functional areas to generate profit. How much of the activity is communicating, processing information and transactions, and research, and how can we change that investment? The category of people also includes supervision and a physical place to work. We will analyze the business to understand how and where we spend our money and what the benefits are by assigning our best possible resources to do the analysis. Once the costs and benefits have been identified and measured, we should challenge the old methodology by considering the benefits of the Web because business changes quickly in this 21st century!

Why can't Mexico steal a march on China? For starters, there's the wage issue. An assembly-line worker in Guadalajara earns $2.50 to $3.50 an hour; his counterpart in Guangdong makes $0.50 to $0.80. Perhaps even more important, China has nurtured large supplier networks in industries such as electronics that Mexico cannot match. The presence of thousands of seasoned Hong Kong and Taiwanese companies on the mainland creates natural partners for multinationals. Besides, China is now a bona fide member of the global trading club, having joined the World Trade Organization (WTO) in 2001. Factor in a 1.3 billion–strong consumer market, and the sum total is too powerful to resist.

That's why companies have deserted Mexico in droves. Employment in the maquiladora industry, the assembly plants that produce primarily for export to the U.S., has dropped nearly 20% from its peak of 1.4 million in 2000, though some losses stem from global economic slowdown.[8]

---

8 "Wasting Away: Despite SARS, Mexico is still losing export ground to China," by Geri Smith, *Business Week,* June 2, 2003, p. 44.

Exhibit 3.1

Financial Summary Alternatives

Alternative Presentations of Selling Expense

	Millions $
Sales	**100.0**
Cost of Sales	45.0
Gross Profit	**55.0**
Selling Expense	**20.0**

Natural Expense

Salaries & Wages	10.0 ⎤
Fringe Benefits	3.0 ⎬ Personnel cash expenditures
Travel	1.0 ⎦
Data Systems	2.0 Nonpersonnel cash expenditures
Depreciation	1.0 Noncash expenditures
Other	3.0
Total	**20.0**

Functional Expense

Selling	14.0
Marketing	2.0
Finance	1.0
Legal	0.5
Other	2.5
Total	**20.0**

Business Category

U.S.	14.0
Latin America	1.0
Europe	2.0
Far East	3.0
Total	**20.0**

The Basic Elements to E-Business Conversion

In order to convert to an *E-nabled* company, we will focus on the basics:

- Leadership
- Team members
- Financial information
- The value chain
- Functions and activities
- Time to complete

Leadership Is Critical—The CEO Owns the Project

Changing the culture of a company to become an e-business will be a very difficult challenge and requires the leadership at the highest level in the company—the chief executive officer (CEO). This is essential because by becoming an e-business, we have added new dimensions to our business by expanding to a global perspective, including all constituents, in a real-time world. Changing to an e-business company will disrupt daily routines, personal responsibilities, and the organization structure itself. It will also require the strongest leaders throughout the company, at every level. We will be unable to convert to an e-business with average personnel or consultants and without the unequivocal sponsorship of the CEO. Experienced leadership is essential because the pace of change requires intuition and sound business judgment. Select the best management to do the work, and you will be grateful for your wisdom.

The conversion to an e-business must be a top priority or it will not be successful. That does not mean that people must be 100 percent dedicated to e-business to the detriment of their current job, but it will require analysis, implementation plans, and timetables that *must be met.*

Personnel fallout—resignations, terminations, demotions, and promotions—as a result of the e-business implementation is inevitable, so be prepared to deal with the difficult challenges. Changes are the result of the global competitive environment, not by internal choices made for the e-business implementation.

Team Members

It is not just a single leader who will make this happen, although the highest leadership is essential. The analysis, planning, and implementation will require the *best people* at every level—no excuses—because this work is the foundation for a renewed global company.

Select the best qualified person for the task even if that person is not a company employee. The company depends on the selection of the best team, so let's be thorough in our assessment of needs and qualifications. Do not just decide on an "established brand" or pedigree (such as PricewaterhouseCoopers [PWC], McKinsey & Company, or Bain & Company); instead, consider how *they* will serve us in this particular task. It pays to also be selfish—assume that our company is the most important client that these consultants will ever serve. In today's global workplace, outside consultants must adapt more to company preferences, and they must work seamlessly with company employees and other consultants as part of their requirements.

Financial Information

The e-business analysis should not be an unnecessarily in-depth financial analysis because global competition demands quick and effective analysis. E-business requires an immediate and perhaps iterative process of analysis-plan-execution. No sense of urgency? Delay the process? You will lose to your global competitors—those competitors who were beyond the horizon only yesterday will take your customers and your best employees today.

Use the existing company financial statements as the foundation for the analysis because the information is readily available and consistently prepared in accordance with generally accepted accounting principles (GAAP). Published financials, prepared according to GAAP, allow comparability of ratios and performance to competitors and other publicly traded entities. Although the analysis will not be perfect, if we wait for the perfect measures and extended studies, we will have lost to the competition.

We will use the basic P&L statement and balance sheet as the foundation for the analysis and then analyze the statements to identify factors that make the company successful. The analysis will include sales analysis, manufacturing cost analysis, and a review of selling, general, and administrative costs to understand where process changes can be made to improve profitability and resource utilization. The analysis can be completed as any large company may do—slowly, ponderously, precisely, all encompassing, and in extraordinary detail—or it can be completed as a scrappy entrepreneur would do. Entrepreneurs get "just enough" information, rely extensively on experience and judgment, and take calculated risks. The e-business analysis should require no more than *12 weeks* to develop initial plans, start execution, and begin to see the results. It is impossible to know everything about the company after only 3 months, but we will have enough information to improve the company value.

We will analyze spending in several ways, such as divisional or business grouping (e.g., consumer products, medical devices, services) or natural P&L categories (e.g., personnel, travel, training). In Exhibit 3.2, we segment the P&L and balance sheet into functional business groups, natural spending categories, or asset and liability classifications. Costs are identified to categories by observation, time study, survey, and management judgment. Accuracy is not critical because timeliness and relative precision are most important. Much of the "nonproduct" spending is based on people costs, as discussed earlier. As you prepare the analysis, it may appear to be overwhelming in the detail, but if you focus on priorities, critical areas and the need for a rapid deployment process, you will see that an effective analysis can be completed in weeks rather than months.

The business value chain will be one view of our business. The value chain consists of primary functions (those that have direct activities to create value, including sales, marketing, operations, etc.) and secondary functions (those necessary to keep the business operating, such as information technology [IT], finance, and legal). Within these functions, it is best to shift costs to the primary functions, which create value by developing or delivering products to the customer. If a company can shift resources from secondary functions to primary functions, sales, earnings, and shareholder value will improve.

The Value Chain of Activities

The e-business analysis will review the value chain from two points of view:

- *Inside the company:* People within the company know their jobs and, with encouragement and guidance, will improve the value chain. The "inside view" concentrates first on the section of value chain unique to your company to determine whether there is a better way to deliver value. For example, in a high-tech company, the product development value chain is much more important than an administrative process such as accounts payable. Although you cannot be successful in a business without timely invoice payment, it is much easier to outsource accounts payable than to develop new products outside the company. Prioritize the analysis on activities, resources used, reporting and tracking processes, and expected outcomes. Inputs to be analyzed should include all resources, whether in-house personnel, contract personnel, outsourced services, assets or liabilities, and the results or outputs of their processes and alternatives.

Exhibit 3.2

Value Chain—Resources and Results

(Millions)

	Consumer Products	Medical Devices	Services	Total Amount	% S/s	Inbound Logistics	Operations	Outbound Logistics	Marketing & Sales	Other
Sales										
Consumer Products	30.0			30.0	23.1%					
Medical Devices		25.0		25.0	19.2%					
Services			75.0	75.0	57.7%					
Total Sales	**30.0**	**25.0**	**75.0**	**130.0**	**100.0%**					
Cost of Sales										
Direct Material				23.0	17.7%	1.0	1.0			21.0
Labor				12.0	9.2%	2.0	9.0	0.5		0.5
Overhead				30.0	23.1%	5.0	18.0	2.0	0.5	4.5
Total Cost				**65.0**	**50.0%**	**8.0**	**28.0**	**2.5**	**0.5**	**26.0**
Gross Margin				**65.0**	**50.0%**		**(28.0)**	**(2.5)**	**(0.5)**	
Selling General & Admin										
Sales										
Personnel										
In-house				16.0	12.3%	0.5		1.0	9.0	5.5
Outsourced				4.0	3.1%		0.5	0.5	3.0	
Advertising				6.0	4.6%	1.0		1.0	4.0	
Travel				2.0	1.5%				2.0	
All other				—	0.0%					
Personnel				12.0	9.3%				5.0	12.0
Other				7.0	5.4%	2.0				
Total SG&A				**47.0**	**36.2%**	**3.5**	**0.5**	**2.5**	**23.0**	
Contribution Margin				**18.0**	**13.8%**					

Functions

44

Cash	10.0					10.0
Inventory	26.0	7.0	7.0	3.0	1.0	7.0
Accounts Receivable	40.0				40.0	
Fixed Assets	25.0	1.0	18.0	0.5	1.0	4.5
Other Assets	5.0					5.0
Total	**105.0**	**8.0**	**25.0**	**3.5**	**42.0**	**26.5**
Accounts Payable	25.0	18.0	3.0	1.0	3.0	
Accruals	5.0	5.0				
Long-Term Debt	10.0	10.0				
Equity	65.0	65.0				
Total	**105.0**	**98.0**	**3.0**	**1.0**	**3.0**	

- *Outside the company:* Global competitive conditions determine performance. What does the customer need? What are the competitor's capabilities? What are our constituents' needs? Constituents are any people or organizations that you interact with, and we should go beyond the current view of constituents and consider *potential constituents.* Customer satisfaction surveys, cycle times, and performance frequency distributions will be measured, tracked, and compared with others. Do not limit yourself to benchmarking performance against only existing competitors; consider anyone performing a similar task in any business anywhere in the world. What was the impact of the automated teller machine (ATM) on consumer finance? In banking, the "best" organizations quickly adopted this product because it provided customer satisfaction—immediate cash available 24 hours a day at virtually any street corner, roadside gas station, or convenience store. Banks that did not consider the new environment added more bank tellers and perhaps extended the normal working hours to improve some of their performance metrics, but they still lost customers. Today, the corner gas station or local convenience store is also a bank, providing the means to pay the bills, transfer cash among accounts and banks, obtain a cash advance, or make a deposit.

We will better understand our value chain investments (tangible, intangible, and personnel assets), funding structures (liabilities and equity), activities and functions, affected constituents, and results of the activity after this initial analysis. The analysis summarizes a basis to measure, plan, and improve potential e-business alternatives. First we will summarize elements of the P&L statement and the balance sheet using function and activity definitions in a matrix. Exhibit 3.2 shows how the basic GAAP and P&L can be presented by function or activity. Once we understand where investments are made today, we can use e-business tools to develop spending alternatives that will increase value (more sales, less cost, and less capital).

Functions and Activities

The primary and secondary functional groupings summarize processes and activities that are used to serve constituents. The functions and activity financial summaries will reflect internal spending (for personnel, travel, training, etc.) and outsourced costs (for people, services, support materials, etc.) and assets/liabilities for the functions. As executives, we invest in

Exhibit 3.3

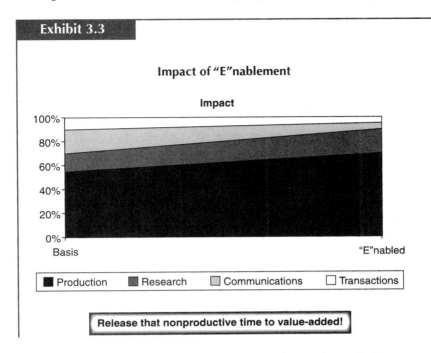

Impact of "E"nablement

Impact

Legend: ■ Production   ■ Research   ▨ Communications   □ Transactions

Release that nonproductive time to value-added!

specific functional areas to improve the firm value, and our decisions are a trade-off between short-term and long-term priorities.

Ideally, we want to redirect firm resources to more productive areas such as research and development (R&D) and improved production processes rather than spend money on internal communications and transaction processing. If well managed, these investments will provide more value to the firm, that is, through improved products, reduced cost, lower capital investment, and so on.

Exhibit 3.3 depicts a business that has shifted 15 percent of available resources to R&D and production from transaction processing and internal communications. The example company has reduced "non-value-added" costs and shifted that investment to more valuable activities. At Mattel Inc., the company concentrated on this primary and secondary trade-off and shifted investment to product development.

Over the past two years, Mattel has cut the time it takes to develop new products by 20%. Paper and clay. When Joe Eckroth took over as Mattel Inc's chief information officer three years ago, he found designers at the company's El Segundo (Calif.) operations snipping and molding prototypes of Barbie dolls and Hot Wheels cars the old-fashioned way. Eckroth promptly moved design online so that virtual models could be zipped electronically to the company's nine factories. That cut development time by 20%.

Eckroth unearthed other savings by putting Mattel's $2 billion licensing pro-
gram online. Instead of shipping all those Barbie backpacks and logoed lunch-
boxes back and forth between Mattel and licensees, the company early this year
digitized and automated the approval process. Now approvals take five weeks
instead of 14. By 2004, Mattel expects all licensees to do business through the
Web, up from 25% now, which should increase revenues by $200 million.[9]

Time Is the Enemy

For a large company, it will take a year or two to complete a detailed functional and natural expense analysis, develop a plan, and begin implementation of the e-business structure. With $10 to $20 million of incremental
spending, anyone can complete these steps. Unfortunately, in a Web-enabled
world, noncompetitive companies that take too long and waste too much
investment destroy value in months and weeks, not years.

Historically, we had months to analyze, plan, and begin execution of the
plan, but today we should begin to see results in weeks. The shift to e-business
should be self-funding over the medium term (less than 12 to 18 months), by
focusing on "quick wins" that create immediate value.

Exhibit 3.4 defines a prototype rapid implementation timeline executing
activities in parallel. The plan is aggressive, because we begin to realize results
within 90 days.

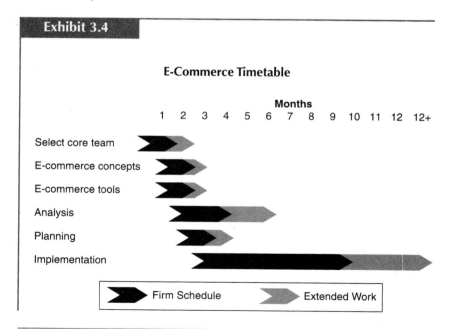

Exhibit 3.4

E-Commerce Timetable

[9] "The WebSmart 50," *Business Week*, November 24, 2003, p. 84.

The Process

The e-business process is an intense, rapid, iterative process that will increase firm value quickly. Critical elements of the e-business process are as follows:

- Select the core team.
- Familiarize the team with the e-business concepts.
- Familiarize the team with preselected tools that stimulate their problem-solving skills.
- Analyze the financial statements and prioritize opportunities.
- Complete the analysis, plan activities, and begin execution.

Each of these topics will be discussed briefly in this chapter and will be more fully explored throughout the remainder of the book.

Select the Core Team

Simply put, the core team must be risk tolerant, creative, goal-oriented, and focused and must have high energy and an indomitable spirit capable of developing solutions beyond the normal constraints of business. The "e-business" team will drive business process change and suffer criticism from many directions about the prioritization and quality of their work. Select the best qualified for the task—both technically and managerially—to ensure that the process is successful. If we do not have the necessary talent within the company, hire consultants from outside, because naysayers will quickly publicize any failure, real or perceived. Limit the risk of failure by planning and executing with only the best personnel.

The e-business leader and team leaders should assess the skill requirements—technical and managerial—to complete the e-business transition as planned. Because of the breadth of skills required, it is best to create a matrix of requirements and then take an inventory of available skills. Skills required will change over time. Exhibit 3.5 lists the skills required (e.g., web page design, hardware expert, accountant, engineer, logistics expertise) as the vertical reference and the time frame (e.g., month 1, 2, 3) as the horizontal legend to assess talent requirements. The talent required will vary from project to project and within the project itself. This is not a precise analysis but rather a rough inventory of existing skills and requirements. Exhibit 3.5 is an example that depicts the strengths and weaknesses of an e-business application and gives the timeframe when critical resources will be required.

Exhibit 3.5

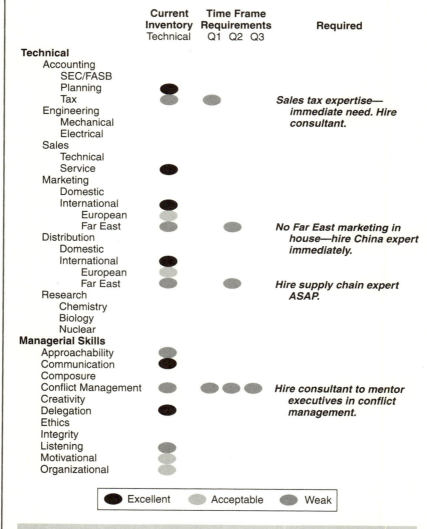

Organizational Assessment: E-Business Capabilities

The functional areas identified represent the most likely areas for improvement based on a preliminary analysis. For example, if a major benefit of "E" is expected in sales operations, break down the sales function to major components and assess the relevant areas.

Familiarize the Team with the "E" Concepts

Because team members will not all be e-business experts, assess their e-business competence by evaluating not only the hardware and software skills but also the nontechnical side of how the Web creates value through instant communications, transaction processing, and research capabilities. Make sure that the team includes e-business experts who understand e-business opportunities and the obstacles and tricks to successful applications. If on-staff experts are available, strategically place these individuals in the teams to provide quicker and more enduring learning. After the team assessment is completed, design an introductory course that discusses case studies, actual results, and the basic advantages of e-business, focused on transaction processing, research, and communications within the most important functional areas. You may also consider visiting an e-business company to see the benefits and risks of becoming *E-nabled*. Organizations that have overcome the hurdles to becoming an e-business are leaders who may like to share their experience with others.

Familiarize the Team with Preselected E-Business Tools

During the training course, use actual examples of software that make a business run more effectively. Include time-saving, labor-saving developmental tools that will be useful in your organization. Salesforce.com, Act, Siebel, Web phone, Webinars, and high-quality sites such as Amazon, Dell, and so forth, will stimulate the participants to identify improvements that can be adapted to the new e-business philosophy. Existing high-quality sites such as Amazon or Dell can be analyzed in advance to improve the experience and focus on relevant aspects of their success.

Analyze the Financial Statements and Prioritize Opportunities

Analyze the company financial statements to identify e-business opportunity. Although GAAP financial statements will be the basis of the analysis, the financials will be modified to reflect nonfinancial values such as time, resources, personnel, products, customers, activities performed, and so forth. Values used in the analysis may not be traditional *hard accounting numbers,* but they will include judgments that have "risk parameters" surrounding each value. Extensive studies and detailed analysis are not necessary, but judgment by the e-business teams is essential to avoid being bogged down in too much detail. We will discuss the analysis techniques in more detail later in this chapter.

Plan and Execute

How often have we heard that companies cannot execute? Unfortunately, in today's e-business world, poor execution will be exposed to the world immediately because results are exposed in real time. Our e-business plans must be clear, concise, and fully accountable, with estimated costs, benefits, and a timeline. The competitive world will harshly judge our performance and will react quickly to slow or ineffective plan execution. Planning in a traditional business can often proceed at a comfortable, internally generated pace, satisfied with sequential step-by-step completion. However, in e-business the tempo is dictated by the competitive environment, which requires multitasking, compressed schedules, and shortcuts whenever feasible. Broadly publicize the e-business plans and share the responsibility with others in the company.

Introduction to Financial Analysis

It is important to be familiar with financial statements because they summarize the business. They tell how and where we have invested, show the current status of investments, and detail the returns on those investments.

Exhibit 3.6 depicts a business environment that consists of inputs/resources and outcomes/results. Inputs are further separated into "P&L" components (expenses or period costs) and balance sheet items (assets, liabilities, and equity). Outcomes/results include summaries of product sales, service sales, orders, delivery statistics, and so on. In an ideal world, the products/services, and so on, will continuously improve while the inputs to generate this flow of products and services will be continuously reduced, improving the company's overall competitiveness.

Financial statements will be recast to concentrate on the business elements that have high current and potential value. Start with the GAAP financial statements, and then, based on discussions with the operation's experts, expand into more meaningful analytical summaries of activity. The analysis will change at every company because their competitive position, investment levels, resources available, and so forth, differ. The goal of the analysis is to find areas to improve value—improve profit, reduce resources required, reduce business cycle time, and so forth.

Analysis

GAAP financial statements include the P&L statement and balance sheet. These statements represent the resources used and the results of operations

Exhibit 3.6

Value Chain—Resources & Results

(Millions $)

Sales	Consumer Products	Medical Devices	Services	Total Amount	% Sls
Consumer Products	30.0			30.0	23.1%
Medical Devices		25.0		25.0	19.2%
Services			75.0	75.0	57.7%
Total Sales	**30.0**	**25.0**	**75.0**	**130.0**	**100.0%**
Cost of Sales					
Direct Material				23.0	17.7%
Labor				12.0	9.2%
Overhead				30.0	23.1%
Total Cost				**65.0**	**50.0%**
Gross Margin				**65.0**	**50.0%**
Selling, General, & Admin					
Sales					
Personnel				28.0	21.5%
Travel				2.0	1.5%
Other				7.0	5.4%
Total SG&A				**37.0**	**28.5%**
Contribution				**28.0**	**21.5%**

Overhead

Inbound Logistics	11.0
Purchasing	3.5
Warehousing	4.5
Training	0.5
Engineering Support	2.5
Supervision	2.0
Communications	1.5
All Other	4.5
Total	**30.0**

Inbound Logistics

Personnel	5.5
Info Tech	0.2
Travel	1.0
Depreciation	1.5
Rent	2.0
Other	0.8
Total	**11.0**

Inbound Logistics

Ordering	1.5
Receiving	2.5
Inspection	4.0
Storing/Location	1.5
Administration	1.0
Other	0.5
Total	**11.0**

(continued)

Exhibit 3.6 *Continued*

Value Chain—Resources & Results

SELLING FUNCTION:
(Ratio as % of Total)

Profile: *Organization:*	#	Assets	Annual *(Millions $)*
Representatives:	200		23.8
Supervisors:	20		3.0
Managers	2		0.5
Sales Executives	1		0.3
Administrative Support	12		0.4
Subtotal	**235**		**28.0**

Assets:
Ten Regional Offices

		Assets	Annual
Laptops		1.0	0.3
Office		0.9	0.2
Automobiles		4.0	1.9
Subtotal		**5.9**	**30.4**

A typical representative spends about 50 hours per week managing current and potential accounts and required internal administration. On average, the rep spends about *10 hours of* "windshield time"; about *8 hours of* "customer research" time per week, including review of financial news and internal account information; and *4 hours per week on internal administration* (sales reporting, expense reports, the administrative tasks). On average, the rep will spend about *2 weeks per year in* "product and sales training," *including 4 days* of travel. The rep allocates time primarily to existing "A" and "B" accounts with little prospecting.

Web Enabled:
- The rep reduced en route travel time 25% based on existing "routing" software.
- The rep reduced customer research time 20% by having internal e-mail alerts when major orders shipped/received and was notified of any "customer event" based on available e-mail alerts driven by Reuters, for example.
- Reduced 50% the amount of internal research using available T&E and CRM (customer resource management) software.
- Reduced offsite travel for training by using Web-based training for products and sales training.
- Based on improved communication (e-mail, net-meetings, etc.), sales management increased their span of control 30%, reducing the supervisory layer 30%.
- The 30% reduction of sales management is shifted to prospecting the 1,500 potential "A" accounts.

and include period costs (expenses) and investments in assets (such as inventory, accounts receivable, or fixed assets). Our objective is to use e-business tools and the creativity of the e-business team to create plans to improve sales, reduce relative cost, and reduce asset investments while becoming more competitive.

To measure progress, we need to know current results, historical trends, and competitive analysis. The financial analysis that we complete will modify the GAAP financials to reflect function, natural expense categories, and activities performed. Later, we will expand the analysis to include possible alternatives to improve the business. We will prioritize the analysis based on judgment and other meaningful information such as market and competitive trends. A rapid analysis cycle time is important to remain competitive.

Exhibit 3.6 shows several forms of the analysis and includes resources consumed and results achieved. Column headings vary based on our objectives, such as understand how we have spent our money categorized by natural expense or perhaps by activity. As we develop the analysis, we will use judgment to focus attention on the most critical elements. The best approach is to move from the largest and most significant *investment and opportunity* to the least significant to avoid wasting time and valuable resources. The selling function has 22 hours of non-value-added time per week driving, administration, research, and so forth, using the Web. Their actual selling time is increased—they are allowed to focus on A and B accounts, and so on.

The cost descriptions represent inputs, which can be defined in several different ways. We want to understand the *types* of inputs and the *size* of investment or commitment and then develop alternatives to these investments based on our knowledge of Internet capabilities. We will look at two examples to demonstrate the process, the first of which is the selling value chain.

Selling Value Chain—Total Cost Is the Key

Total cost is the key because any individual cost component may be reduced but overall cost may increase in response to changes made. For example, if buying a component from California can save 1 percent of the material cost but we must pay the freight, total cost may not be lower. Also in Exhibit 3.6, total overhead represents 23 percent of the product cost—the single largest component. In the example, overhead will include the entire support infrastructure required to prepare an acceptable quality and quantity of product for customer sale. When we consider overhead elements, we will find costs such as depreciation, service costs, personnel (direct and indirect), utilities, supplies, IT, and so on. Each of these costs should be summarized and prioritized for review to determine whether we can save the cost or somehow improve value from the investment. It is not important if some of these costs are already "sunk costs"—such as capital investments, which will result in depreciation. If a machine is no longer required because we expand capacity through efficiencies, there is an opportunity to either dispose of the equipment, creating cash flow; or to use the equipment in another process; or possibly even to outsource the excess capacity. Each scenario will create company value.

Referring again to Exhibit 3.6, notice how much selling general and administrative cost relates to personnel, travel, and advertising. Each of these spending categories can be challenged using the new e-business paradigm to improve utilization, reduce overall costs, or improve the process. Again, through prioritization based on value, challenge the status quo and substitute new e-business activities whenever possible.

The Approach

Start the analysis with the highest level of financial data available. Some companies are organized in divisions based on customer segment/market and perhaps further segmented by product type or geographic region. When first developing the matrix, carefully consider the implications of the initial segmentation because some hidden factors may be exactly the opportunities that will create value. For example, if a company is organized by division based on product line, advantages of geographic organization may be missed.

Candidly discuss the business with executives and the people who actually do the work—they are experts. Focus on business inputs and outputs and the potential benefit of change using e-business techniques. There will be certain facts identified, hypotheses speculated, and some extreme brainstorming assumptions made that will need more analysis. The analytical process will consider inputs, whether in-house or outsourced, and will challenge each of the major assumptions about how we manage the company so that we are certain that no major opportunity is missed.

Eventually the entire company value chain will be analyzed, regardless of the current investments, because if we examine only what is here today, we will never explore what could be. If a company has historically avoided outsourcing, outsourcing payroll processing could be a missed opportunity. The following questions should be posed:

- What are we doing today? *Our goal is to increase value, not just reduce cost.* As we examine the costs and investments, we should not look only to eliminate tasks, but we should aggressively challenge how we can invest to get more benefit. If we eliminate tasks in customer service, what else can these people do to create value?

- What are we missing? As we look at the business, think about methods that have never been used before to increase value. If Amazon.com considered their job to be only one of satisfying order demand, they would miss major cross-selling and expense reduction opportunities. By understanding how the actual customer and the browsing customer shop, Amazon.com sells more, at less overall cost. Amazon has invested in database management to guide the customer by suggesting, "Customers who bought this book also bought . . ." Amazon has also managed the order-processing costs by suggesting that, ". . . if you purchase $x.xx more, you will receive free shipping," thus reducing the overall cost of doing business. They have learned to increase value by understanding their role in the buying decision.

As we examine the example P&L and the balance sheet, we have modified some of the descriptions to reflect "groups" of costs. For example, personnel costs represent all costs associated with personnel—such as payroll, bonus, vacation, health care, life insurance, training, and so on. We group costs by functional driver to avoid missing costs that may be captured in other functional areas—for example, training costs may be captured in the human resources function.

For the initial analysis, use the value streams described by Michael Porter in his book *Competitive Advantage: Creating and Sustaining Superior Performance,* which can represent any company. These include the following:

Primary Activities:
- Inbound logistics
- Operations
- Outbound logistics
- Marketing and sales
- Service

Support Activities:
- Firm infrastructure
- Human resources management
- Technology development
- Procurement

Each of the functions—both primary and support—includes investments in activities, tangible and intangible assets, and liabilities that support the business. We will analyze the inputs or resource requirements among these categories. The first level of analysis would include the asset categories and other inputs such as people, expense, and outsourced services.

Examples—Analysis

Selling Value Chain   Product line sales are affected by the competition, product design, quality, delivery pricing, and so forth. As we analyze the inputs in the selling value chain, we will identify all the elements of cost—personnel, materials, service costs, depreciation, and so on. We should identify major investment areas because the largest investments will often yield the greatest value. It is not necessary to examine every product, cost component, or activity; instead, concentrate on what is most important (e.g., competitors, customers, vendors, regulations). Use a Pareto analysis—ranking from most important to least important—to identify analysis target areas. This will help avoid too much analysis, which will slow the process and may result in opportunities being missed. Assign the best people to the project because they can substitute their informal knowledge and intuition about the business for extensive detailed analysis.

In Exhibit 3.7, the sales representative spends more than 50 percent of his time on activities other than direct selling. Using e-business techniques, his nonselling time will be reduced. Keys to the redeployment to more value-added activities will be, for example, e-mail notices of the status of major orders, which eliminate research time by the sales representative; Webinars, which eliminate the need for travel to a single location for training; and online routing software, which optimizes windshield time.

Example—Inbound Logistics

Inbound logistics includes activities such as creating, reviewing, and approving a forecast and assessing inventory levels and existing orders and backorders. Exhibit 3.6 also shows an example of the several activities (order,

Exhibit 3.7

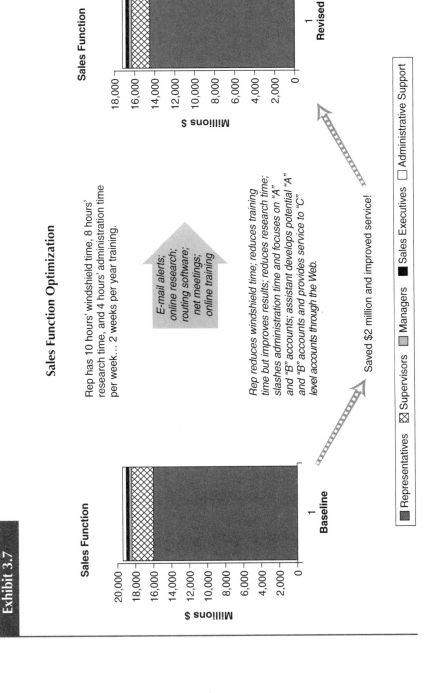

Sales Function Optimization

Sales Function

Rep has 10 hours' windshield time, 8 hours' research time, and 4 hours' administration time per week... 2 weeks per year training.

E-mail alerts; online research; routing software; net meetings; online training

Rep reduces windshield time; reduces training time but improves results; reduces research time; slashes administration time and focuses on "A" and "B" accounts; assistant develops potential "A" and "B" accounts and provides service to "C" level accounts through the Web.

Saved $2 million and improved service!

Sales Function

Millions $

18,000
16,000
14,000
12,000
10,000
8,000
6,000
4,000
2,000
0

1
Revised

Millions $

20,000
18,000
16,000
14,000
12,000
10,000
8,000
6,000
4,000
2,000
0

1
Baseline

■ Representatives ☒ Supervisors ■ Managers ■ Sales Executives □ Administrative Support

59

inspection, etc.) that are required to perform the traditional inbound logistics function.

The exhibit lists several steps required, the actual activity time required, and the elapsed time required to do the steps. In an e-business, using *Lean* techniques (i.e., eliminate non-value-added activities, optimize processes), the number of steps required, the time required to complete each step, and the elapsed time to complete the process will each be reduced. Using Web technology, the communications, research, and transaction time will be condensed to improve performance.

We will also see efficiencies in the P&L inputs such as people, fringe benefits, insurance, interest, outsourced service costs, depreciation, and so forth, while investments in accounts receivable, inventory, fixed assets, and so on, should be reduced. Customer satisfaction should improve (customers will receive improved products and services faster, and more complete and accurate information that will improve their efficiency and overall profitability); vendors will be more effective, efficient, and profitable; and our shareholders will enjoy increased wealth because our organization will become more effective.

> *The Project: To analyze 60,000 orders daily to figure out how many Teamsters it needs at its 325 facilities. The Payoff: By calculating the employees needed, the company saves $100 million a year. From the outside, Yellow Corp. hasn't changed much since 1926. That is when A.J. Harrell added freight shipping to his Yellow Cab business in Oklahoma City. But these days, Yellow runs on a thick stream of digital data that's almost as vital as diesel fuel. Yellow Corp. uses E-Business extensively to reduce non-value added time and improve overall profitability.*
>
> *Every day, the trucking giant receives some 60,000 orders over the Internet or at its call centers. While other trucking companies do that, Yellow goes further. It feeds all that data into a proprietary computer program to plot down to the person, how many drivers it will need during the four shifts at every one of its terminals the next day. . . . That's quite a juggling act, involving 19,300 Teamsters and 8,250 trucks at 335 facilities across the U.S.*[10]

Example—Balance Sheet

Assets   Noncash assets are often immovable and less liquid than cash, and if not invested wisely, they may have a carrying cost as well as an

---

[10] "The WebSmart 50," *Business Week,* November 24, 2003, p. 100.

opportunity cost far in excess of interest. The carrying cost will be the lowest borrowing rate at which your company can borrow, and the opportunity cost can be virtually unlimited. As an example, we have accounts receivable of $40 million from a normal sales cycle—receive an order, either manufacture to order or ship from inventory, and deliver to customer. If we could accelerate the selling and order fulfillment process, we could accelerate the payment process because we are creating value for the customer. What if we can save other costs for customers, such as shipping, storage, obsolescence, and other handling costs? Will they share some of those savings with us?

A quick review of the value chain shows that by downloading the scanned off-the-shelf inventory movement, orders can be restocked without any manual intervention, reducing the administrative time, accelerating the restocking process, and allowing us to better schedule the production operation. By using selected LTL (less than truckload) vendors such as Yellow Corp., we can also monitor the shipment progress as it crosses the United States. The store can track the inventory through a website to have exact shipping information available for its delivery or customer service department, which can schedule the installation of the product to smooth the workload. This also provides the customer with a competitive advantage because, conceivably, with 4 days' stock on hand (the normal cycle time for an LTL shipment in the example), the store will never be out of stock. Emergency shipments can also be handled through airfreight or other priority shipping. In exchange for all this additional service, which saves them money, ask for permission to debit their accounts when the shipment is made, thereby reducing our financial exposure but also providing premium service in return, at no additional cost.

Inventory

If we could lower our inventory levels and improve service to our customers, would we do it? Less investment in inventory will mean lower obsolescence cost, less working capital requirements, reduced warehouse and handling costs, improved service levels, and more free cash flow for other areas of investment. Inventories can be reduced through online reporting and production scheduling—if the information is available remotely through customers or sales representatives, the buying decision can be simplified. Amazon.com and Dell manage their inventories through direct links to their manufacturers, who maintain the inventory. Products are ordered through the Amazon.com or Dell customer interface and then directly shipped through a standardized, common carrier process, such as UPS (United Parcel Service), which has online order tracking. Amazon and Dell have substituted technology for inventory levels and bricks and mortar.

Each of these examples substitutes immediate information and instant transaction processing for investments in hard assets. Examine the activity in any e-company and you will find major investments in communications, transactions processing, and research—not physical production of goods.

If 60 percent of your spending is for personnel-related services, think about the tangible product and production activities that you perform. When we analyze the assets, liabilities, and personnel in our company, we will find that a significant part of the company activity is not spent producing the tangible product. In fact, when we consider the Web as a productivity-enhancing tool, we may also challenge "production" processes that we perform because we have access to almost any production facility anywhere in the world through the Web and outsourcing. That being said, will you do business the same as you did last year or last month? Or would you outsource or change the source of some or all of the production to somewhere else in the United States, Latin America, China, or perhaps even Africa. In today's economy, the best executives think outside the four walls of the company, outside the borders of the country, and well beyond the visible horizon.

Regardless of what the numerous software vendors demand, it is unnecessary to invest in an entirely new system to engage in e-business. The smartest people analyze their needs and selectively implement software enhancements that will benefit them most. In some applications, it is not even necessary to invest in entire enterprise resource planning (ERP) packages because many of the critical services are available on an *a la carte* basis. We will have to become more familiar with the software first.

Summary

We have now discussed the type of analysis required and a process that challenges every function and activity that the company performs. This is the framework for a successful e-business project, and the task has just begun. In the next chapter, we will thoroughly explore the functions, activities, and constituents included in any company.

CHAPTER 4

ASSESSMENT—FUNCTIONS

Introduction

During the past 10 years the Web has evolved from an exclusive domain for technical experts to a tool that is integral in our personal and business lives. We would never have believed that the Internet would become as indispensable as the telephone. We have all used the Web and the Internet for years to improve our communication, speed our research, and process transactions seamlessly across the world. But when was the last time that we pondered the Web as a strategic tool to make our business a stronger global competitor? When did we last consider the "global" concept for our business by thinking beyond existing strictures? This chapter will introduce the Web as a strategic tool to improve our company's performance. We will discuss specific ways to analyze our business and examples of ways to use the Web to improve our company's value. We will first define today's business using spending by functional area as the basis, discuss business drivers, and finally brainstorm some alternatives that have been used by others to improve their company's performance. By the end of this chapter, we will have identified analytical approaches and investment opportunities that can be implemented.

The Web Is a Tool

Twenty-five years ago, the Apple computer quietly infiltrated the business community—not the information technology (IT) community—by delivering an essential service that never before existed. Immediate, flexible, easily modified *electronic spreadsheets* supplanted reams of multicolumned accountants worksheets, Number 2 pencils, and electronic calculators. And the businessperson did this without the intrusion of the IT experts. The Apple computer was *user friendly,* and it changed the *pace of business.*

Twenty-five years ago, Fred Smith had an idea that *overnight delivery* was an essential competitive element of a well-run global company. FedEx was born to a skeptical business community, and it not only survived but thrived and created an entirely new, multibillion dollar industry. Overnight delivery changed the *pace of business.*

These were not *strategies* but rather tools that were developed to meet the unseen needs of the business community. Then in the mid-1990s, the Web was born. Once again, like the Apple computer and overnight delivery, the *Web* is a tool used to accelerate the pace of business. However, the Web also has an impact on the breadth of business, affecting *every country*—no matter how poor—*potentially every business*—no matter whether tangible goods or service—and *every function.*

The Internet and the Web may now be a part of any global strategy because businesses require *people* to complete *transactions*—creating something of value for the customer. Progressive business leaders embraced the tool and created entirely new competitive strategies around the Web, regardless of their size! Consider the following:

- Amazon.com has broadened its product lines well beyond books to include *consumer electronics, clothing, used books, recorded music and videos,* and *kitchen and housewares.* Special shopping sites have also been established for *Germany, Japan, the United Kingdom, Canada, France,* and *Spain.*
- The local car dealer now notifies the customer by e-mail when the car should be serviced, runs promotions to balance the service area workload, and competes with a broader market to include regional or perhaps national new and used car dealers to sell vehicles.
- Medtronic, Inc., now offers *remote heart monitoring* to more than 4,000 of its patients. Patients simply hold a small electronic antenna over their chest to transmit data to a doctor via a standard telephone line.[11]
- The independent trucker minimizes or eliminates non-revenue-producing runs by accessing a website and securing backhaul loads on a real-time basis to generate incremental revenue.

In each case, the Web has become a part of the strategy to improve value, regardless of size, industry, or location. Because there are very few size or industry constraints, competitors can easily integrate the Web into their business and try to steal business from others.

As we have seen, the car dealer, the independent trucker, and the multi-billion dollar companies all have developed ways to use the Web to improve value. These Web applications do not necessarily require technology experts to become enabled but rather a businessperson to assess the available Web tools, focus on value creation through their opportune use, and capture the

---

[11] "Physicians Now Can Use the Internet to Remote Monitor Patients with Heart Failure," Medtronic, Inc. Press Release, December 22, 2003.

value. In the cases cited, the value was either *improved customer service*—an invaluable competitive weapon—*improved asset utilization*—a way to improve their cost structure and increase sales—or *expanded sales reach*—promotion through the Web. They identified a need, matched an available tool, and adapted and integrated the tool into their business processes.

In Exhibit 4.1, the independent trucker identified an underutilized asset and used the Web to eliminate downtime, increase revenue, and improve overall profitability by matching availability to real-time transportation requirements. No long-term contracts, no significant downtime, only increased revenue with minimal out-of-pocket costs.

Define the Business—Summarize Resources

On the surface, it is easy to say that our business is, for example, to simply sell the *widget* to the customer. However, for the e-business analysis, we should expand the definition to say that we exist to *serve the customer* (current or potential), with a *product/service* (current or potential), in a given *geography* (current or potential) through trade *channels* (current or potential), using *processes* (current or potential) and an *organization* (current or potential) to beat the *competitors* (current or potential) to make a fair profit. We complete these tasks through the organization, which includes many different functions.

We will define our business in a structured way by first examining the functions performed in the company and then in the next chapter examining the activities performed within the functions. Once we have defined the business, we will brainstorm to identify ways to improve our existence. We will review primary and secondary functions in the following sections.

Primary and Support Functions

Primary and support functions are thoroughly discussed in Michael Porter's book *Competitive Performance: Creating and Sustaining Competitive Performance.* A brief explanation follows for your reference:

- Primary functions are those used to directly compete in the marketplace; they include areas such as operations, selling, marketing, and so forth.
- Support functions are those that make it possible to run the company in a competitive environment, such as finance, legal, human resources, and so forth.
- Some functions perform *direct activities*—activities that actually create or deliver a product or service to the customers, such as producing a

Exhibit 4.1

Trucking Analysis

	Pre-Internet	Post-Internet	Notes
Cost/Hour	70	70	
Revenue/Hour—Peak	140	140	
Revenue/Hour—Off-peak	110	110	
Hours Billed—Peak	1,350	1,350	
Hours Billed—Off-peak	-	300	Hours billed off-peak represent backhaul revenue, which would not be realized without the Web.
Revenue			
Peak	189,000	189,000	
Off-peak	-	33,000	Hours billed off-peak represent backhaul revenue, which would not be realized without the Web.
Total Revenue	189,000	222,000	
Cost of Sales	94,500	94,500	
Gross Profit	94,500	127,500	Gross profit increased by 100% of the off-peak revenue because the backhaul would have been completed without the backhaul booking. This was necessary to reposition the truck at the correct debarkation point.
Gross Profit % of Sales	50%	57%	

In this example, the hauler uses the Internet to schedule backhaul loads that ordinarily would be nonrevenue producing. Off-peak billings are less per hour to share the savings/benefit with the vendor and build relationships that may expand the business.

tangible product—whereas other functions perform *indirect activities*—for example, providing a necessary support product or service such as a payroll processing operation to ensure that the customer is better served.

We will discuss activities more thoroughly in the next chapter. To be effective in a very competitive e-business world, we should identify the functions that can have the greatest impact on value, regardless of their current impact on today's business, and implement programs to capture that value.

As an example, a sales department serves a primary function—selling to existing and potential customers. To do this effectively, the department includes sales representatives (direct activity of selling) and administrative personnel to manage internal information, schedule meetings, purchase office supplies, and prepare budgets (indirect activities). This analysis will examine all functions and activities and categorize how we use our resources, before we brainstorm for improvement.

Primary and support functions are performed in every company, although in some companies selected functions (i.e., inbound logistics in a bank) have minimal impact on company value. Create a matrix of functions performed in the company and the resources used in these functional areas as a first step to define the business. All functional areas should be considered in the analysis, although the impact on profitability and value creation will vary based on industry, products, and stage of company growth.

Summarize the resources used first from published financial and other management data and then group them as expenses, capital (including all assets used in the business), and personnel (permanent, temporary, and contract personnel). Precision is not critical in the summary, *but all resources used in the company should be assigned.* The matrix will include all the functional areas in the company, with descriptive notes that will be helpful in the brainstorming part of the analysis. Expenses, capital, and so on, will be assigned to a function based on actual work completed, surveys, observations of department activity, and so forth.

Usually, the analysis is completed on an iterative basis because complete data may not be readily available for the initial summary. Use judgment and do not postpone the analysis if the information is substantially complete. We can continue the analysis to the next steps using an "open items list" for follow-up later. Also, if there have been recent significant changes in company spending, prepare a summary comparing several periods of financial data to better understand the trends.

Depending on the size and breadth of the company, this iterative analysis should be prepared within 10 days of start for companies with sales of less

Exhibit 4.2

Opportunity Analysis

(Millions $)

Function	$ Expenses		Capital			Other Invest.	Personnel Resources		
	Direct	Indirect	M&E	Real Prop	Other		In-house	Outsourced	Total
Primary									
Inbound Logistics									
Operations									
Outbound Logistics									
Marketing & Sales									
Service									
Support									
Firm Infrastructure									
Human Resource Management									
Technology Development									
Procurement									
Inbound Material Handling									
Inbound Inspection									
Inbound Transportation									
Total									

Note: All functional activities within a given function have not been represented on this worksheet but should be documented when a company is being analyzed.

Note: This worksheet and similar worksheets should be prepared for each department, location, or business segment in the company. When completed, you may find that certain functions are performed by departments other than in the particular functional area. For example, it is not unusual to find that procurement—ordering is performed in most departments, even if only for items limited to office supplies, small equipment items, and so forth.

Totals on the master company worksheet should equal the total company investments—approximately. Precision is not as important as efficiently completing the analysis.

than $500 million and somewhat longer as company size and complexity increase. Regardless of company size, the analytical project should be staffed so that the initial analysis can be completed in 30 days or less to keep the *pace* of the project on track.

Process to Summarize

First define whether the company is highly centralized or decentralized to prioritize the analysis. *Centralized* or *highly functionalized* companies should review the functions centrally from the top down to identify the critical functions that will provide the most benefit to the company. For example, if a major financial institution has centralized functions for human resources, IT, credit card operations, and so forth, the analysis should concentrate on investments and opportunities defined within this structure, or in a way that is consistent with the normal operations. However, if during the analysis it is apparent that decentralization is best for the company, the analysis can be used to facilitate the reorganization.

Decentralized operations may be self-contained with all or most functional areas represented in each operation. If autonomous operations exist, it is often easier to develop e-business applications within the business unit because the application may be smaller under a single leadership group. If there is a strategic need for a more centralized company, e-business may actually facilitate the centralization process because communications are instant and consistent and standards can be established across many units. Executive judgment about the strategic goal will determine the best approach to e-business because the analysis will vary with every business.

If we consider size of investment as our first method of prioritization, the investments listed in Exhibit 4.3 would focus us on operations in the centralized company because this represents the largest investment opportunity. In Exhibit 4.3, in a decentralized operation, you may consider concentrating on the Miami region, again because it has the largest concentration of investment. However, be careful not to use cost as the only measure to prioritize opportunity because we are looking for value, which may not be based on spending levels.

This kind of analysis should be completed for each of the major functions within our company. A listing of example functions follows. Although each of the functions should be considered carefully in the analysis, not all functions should be modified using the e-business platform.

Exhibit 4.3

Opportunity Analysis

Centralized Expenses—Direct

(Millions $) Function	Headquarters	Cincinnati	Atlanta	Chicago	Miami	Total
Primary						
Inbound Logistics	15					15
Operations	75					75
Outbound Logistics	12					12
Marketing & Sales	4	9	11	15	22	61
Service	22	1	1	0	2	26
Support						
Firm Infrastructure	24	1			1	26
Human Resource Management	11					11
Technology Development	37					37
Procurement	2					2
Total	202	11	12	15	25	265

Decentralized Expenses—Direct

(Millions $) Function	Headquarters	Cincinnati	Atlanta	Chicago	Miami	Total
Primary						
Inbound Logistics		3	2	4	6	15
Operations	4	12	15	20	24	75
Outbound Logistics		2	3	3	4	12
Marketing & Sales	4	9	11	15	22	61
Service		3	3	4	16	26
Support						
Firm Infrastructure	4	4	5	4	9	26
Human Resource Management	2	2	2	2	3	11
Technology Development	5	2	4	4	22	37
Procurement	2					2
Total	21	37	45	56	106	265

Primary:
- Operations
- Outbound logistics
- Marketing and sales
- Marketing management
- Advertising
- Sales force administration
- Sales force operations
- Technical literature
- Promotions
- Service

Support Functions:
- Procurement
- Human resources management
- Technology development
- Firm infrastructure
- Accounting
- Tax compliance
- Tax strategy
- Legal
- Intellectual property
- Treasury

Each line of the matrix represents a functional area that is a part of the total company matrix. Headings across the top represent the major resource categories—dollars or head count. Additional worksheets should be developed to give more detail about each of the functions and to support the total company analysis. For example, the inbound logistics function may include subfunctions such as receiving, inspection, storing, and so forth. These additional worksheets will be in a format that is similar to the company master worksheets—that is, they will define the function/subfunction performed and summarize the resources required to perform the function.

Resource analysis is challenging because resources are often categorized into specific divisions and/or functions (e.g., sales, marketing, research and development [R&D]) but may often perform more than one function. For example, proper personnel classification by function may be difficult because people may be identified with a location or broad definition of responsibility, but the people may actually perform several functions. In some companies, clerical staff in the administration—accounting function may actually purchase office supplies and travel. Initially, these *people* costs would be classified as infrastructure—accounting until the reviewer identified their day-to-day activities as purchasing and allocated that portion of cost to purchasing. Similar misclassifications may exist for assets and expenses. Survey the people actually working in the departments to identify the major functional classifications. A description of the components of an example worksheet follows:

- *Costs:* This category includes all spending, such as personnel costs, rent, IT, travel, supplies, and so forth, broken into direct and indirect spending categories. Activity costs will be discussed more thoroughly in the next chapter.
  - *$ Expenses—direct:* These costs represent spending to create value for the buyer or customer for activities such as manufacturing and assembly, selling research, product design, and so forth.
  - *$ Expenses—indirect:* These costs represent other costs incurred to *support* the direct activities; examples include administrative functions, maintenance, accounting, facility management, and so forth.
- *Capital—machinery and equipment (M&E):* These are the total *net investment* (cost less accumulated depreciation) in M&E to support the function; examples include assets used exclusively in the particular function and allocated assets that are used to complete the function. Allocated assets are those assets that are used by more than one function—for example, computer systems in the IT function. Although it is reasonable to allocate assets for the analysis, be sure to make decisions about improved performance based only on discrete investments; that is, it may be difficult to dispose of part of a computer system to improve your cash flow and reduce your assets if the system is used by other functions.
- *Capital—buildings/real estate, and so forth:* These capital costs represent the current net book value of the assets (cost less accumulated depreciation) used in a particular function. Again, allocations are acceptable, but be careful when you consider disposition of assets.
- *Capital—other:* This category includes net intangible assets (cost basis less accumulated amortization), such as customer lists, patents, goodwill, software, and so forth.
- *Other investments:* These assets include any assets not otherwise classified, such as deposits, prepaid items, inventory, and so forth.

- *Personnel—inside:* This category represents the number of employees and related costs to perform functions.
- *Personnel—outsourced:* These represent the full-time equivalents and cost of personnel performing the functions by outside organizations. The metrics may be difficult to obtain but once again use judgment to capture the information as quickly and practically as possible.

As we continue to change our company and become more enabled, these individual investments may decline because we may reduce or eliminate entire processes or shift the activities to the vendors, ideally while sharing the benefits with the vendors—such as faster cycle time, minimal obsolescence, shrinkage, and so forth.

After we make all the adjustments among the functions and spending categories, the financials may not agree exactly with the detailed published financial information. Once the differences are properly reconciled and all the costs and assets are summarized, the analysis is complete. All *resources*—costs, assets, people, and outsourcing—should be assigned to functional areas and subjected to the brainstorming process.

Identify the Drivers

Once the functional resources have been identified, we should identify the *cost drivers*. "Cost drivers are the structural causes of the cost of an activity and can be more or less under a firm's control."[12]

Cost drivers are thoroughly discussed in Porter's book and include the following:

- Economies of scale—activities are more efficient at larger scale.
- Learning—cost reductions that result from improved knowledge.
- Pattern of capacity utilization—based on long-term performance.
- Linkages—coordination of potentially linked activities can change cost.
- Interrelationships—sharing knowledge among business units may change cost structures.
- Integration—extent of vertical integration may change cost structure.
- Timing—timing of business activity within a business cycle may affect firm cost structure.
- Discretionary policies—policy decisions may have a major impact on cost (e.g., quality standards, performance standards, markets served).

---

[12] "Competitive Advantage: Creating and Sustaining Superior Performance," by Michael E. Porter, The Free Press, 1985, New York.

- Location—includes both strategic (countries with operations) and tactical (e.g., cities, buildings) considerations.
- Institutional factors—such as regulatory matters governed by the U.S. Food and Drug Administration (FDA), the Federal Trade Commission (FTC), customs and immigration requirements, and so on.

A quick review of just the titles allows you to understand the kind of impact that e-business might have on your business.

As an example, let's examine several drivers within an inbound logistics function to see how we can change the activity using the Web, focusing on communications, research, and transaction processing:

- Review the *pattern of capacity utilization* to manage the flow of product received to our business. If the capacity utilization can be smoothed using e-business, fewer resources will be required, overall costs will be reduced, and firm value will be increased. Leveled capacity utilization by managing demand through the Web will also effectively increase the throughput, potentially increasing sales, customer service, and profitability. This phenomenon is not limited to manufacturing operations. "At the University of Central Florida, in Orlando, President John C. Hitt has launched an all-out campaign for efficiency in the face of dwindling state support and a doubling of enrollment in a decade, to nearly 40,000. Classrooms, which sit empty much of the day at many colleges, are now used from 7:30 AM to 10 PM. That helped the space crunch, as did Web-enhanced courses that meet just once a week and require most work to be done online. . . . The payoff? UCF spends just 4.4% of its core academic and administration budget on operations and maintenance, vs. the 7%-plus common at comparable public universities."[13]
- *Linkages to suppliers* will be explored. Linkage changes may provide mutual benefits to both suppliers and our company. By changing the linkages in areas such as product design, just-in-time (JIT) shipping, or cross-docking capabilities, we may actually cede control over a portion of our value chain but improve performance. TAL Apparel Ltd., a closely held Hong Kong shirt maker, collects point-of-sale information directly from JC Penney stores, processes the information through a proprietary computer model, and actually manufactures and ships products directly to each JC Penney store, completely bypassing the

---

[13] "Colleges in Crisis," by William C. Symonds, *Business Week*, April 28, 2003, pp. 71–79.

retailer's warehouses. "Before it started working with TAL a decade ago, Penney would routinely hold up to six months of inventory in its warehouses and three months' worth at stores. Now, for the Stafford and Crazy Horse shirt lines that TAL handles, 'it's zero'...."[14]

- *Interrelationships* within our business and with outside business units can be explored as a means of increasing value. E-business processes have enabled collaboration among company suppliers and among company business units to share value-added activity, reduce overall costs, and improve value. By better understanding a company or organization, existing interrelationships can be exploited. For example, at Harvard University the various schools historically operated independently. A recent study by McKinsey & Company identified potential savings for the university of up to $30 million simply by consolidating its purchasing power. "So Harvard brought its law, business, and other schools together to seek competitive bids for all their computer equipment, a contract won by IBM that will save Harvard $3 million a year."[15]

- *Improved timing or business pace* will be a benefit captured through e-business and inbound logistics. Effective inbound logistics may change the entire value chain by no longer requiring merchandise receiving at our company, thereby reducing total investment and stock-keeping losses for shrinkage and obsolescence. This can also accelerate the pace of order fulfillment and prove to be a killer application in a competitive environment, just as Dell and Amazon.com have done.

- *Location* of the inbound logistics function can be a tremendous benefit to a company. Once again, consider that Amazon.com may never take possession of a product before it is shipped and billed to the customer. They have totally eliminated an entire cost layer within the value chain. Dell also uses similar inbound logistics techniques to improve their competitive value position.

Brainstorm Opportunities for the Functions

Thus far we have summarized where we invest and have also identified the cost drivers within major functional areas. Brainstorming armed with these

---

[14] "Made to Measure: Invisible Supplies Has Penney's Shirts All Buttoned Up," by Gabriel Kahn, *The Wall Street Journal*, online, September 11, 2003.

[15] "Colleges in Crisis," by William C. Symonds, *Business Week*, April 28, 2003, pp. 70–79.

facts and earlier exposure to e-business processes will allow us to identify potential applications for improvement. As opportunities are identified, rank the benefit to the company, including cost to implement and probability of success. Relative priority will depend on the company's strategic requirements when the analysis is completed. If a company is *cash poor,* priority rankings may be focused on cash generation capabilities, or perhaps cost and time to implement. If sales force utilization is a priority in a cash-poor company, Salesforce.com may be an ideal application for immediate benefit. The application is quick to implement, with little up-front implementation cost, providing an immediate benefit. Of course, the downside of such an application systems provider (ASP) application may be that over the long term, the application may not be robust enough to sustain the company. The executive team must understand the current benefits and make trade-offs.

The brainstorming process should require 1 to 2 days of focused discussion to define the potential "e" applications. It is important to have all executives participate because cross-functional costs/benefits may be developed during the brainstorming. Brainstorming results will fall into two categories:

- *In-the-box,* incremental solutions that do not require radical changes in the business process and may be easily and inexpensively implemented. Examples include establishing policy changes that require using e-mail rather than hard-copy paper mail; using Web meetings instead of travel whenever possible; and using single source, approved vendors for commodity purchases such as office supplies or basic materials. These simple, low-cost opportunities for value improvement require little incremental expense spending, capital spending, or personnel to support the e-business application, and the benefits will fund additional e-business initiatives to improve overall company performance.
- *BHAG*-kind of developments. *BHAG* is a term originally used by Jim Collins to discuss *Big Hairy Audacious Goals.*[16] Break the mold concepts—things out of the ordinary that may prove to be extremely valuable to the company but may also be expensive and complex to implement. Estimated costs and benefits for these developments will initially have less credibility because these investment areas may never have been considered before. Consider changing any or all the major variables that are now used to create, manufacture, promote, sell, and

---

16 "On the edge with Jim Collins," by Jim Collins, interview with Tom Brown, *Industry Week,* October 5, 1992.

distribute today's products and services. Who could imagine a successful trade show presence without rigid displays, hundreds of square feet of dedicated floor space, and thousands of dollars of travel and entertainment expenses. "For exhibitors, running a booth is far cheaper online than at traditional shows. A booth at EE Times' System on Chip show costs anywhere from $3,000 to $20,000, with exhibitors paying more for more prominent placement, brighter colors or more options for linking to products or press releases. Trillium, a unit of Harte-Hanks Inc. of San Antonio, Texas, pays $55,000 annually to be a charter sponsor at dataWarehouse.com's four shows a year, which works out to less than the $16,000 it spends on average for a booth at a single offline show. What's more, there are no travel, hotel or shipping expenses—not to mention the cost of hosting a party. For some exhibitors, such costs can inflate the tab for an offline show to as much as $500,000. . . . Nearly 40% of dataWarehouse.com's visitors are from outside the U.S., with India, the United Kingdom and the Benelux countries represented most."[17]

Some BHAG examples follow:

- Expand the ethnic marketing of company products and services by marketing on the Web in Spanish or another language.
- Add telemarketing to the marketing mix, using the Web and an internal database as the foundation for targeted promotions based on customer demographics, order patterns, trade channels, and so forth.
- Add the top-selling products that represent 80 percent of the value that you now sell to the Web offering, thereby reducing operating costs.
- Sell the bottom 20 percent of products only through the Web, reducing operating costs, and share the savings with the customers.
- Solicit customer feedback on the company Web page to obtain real-time, unbiased information about products and services and also to ensure feedback from the customer.

Do not spend more than 1 to 2 days on this first iteration of both the "in-the-box" and BHAG brainstorming. After the initial brainstorming is completed, apply sensitivity analysis to test the validity of your estimates with the people in the organization to ensure that the initial cost/benefit estimates

---

[17] "The Show Goes On," by Jennifer Saranow, Special Report: E-Commerce, *The Wall Street Journal,* online, April 28, 2003.

are not too far afield. A quick summary is tabulated in Exhibit 4.4. Note the high order of magnitude of the summary, which will visually help prioritize the benefits.

When we are done tabulating the results of the brainstorming, we will have a list of potential activities that initially will have a net cost but that will eventually lead to significant value improvements for the firm.

Exhibit 4.5 (p. 82) is an example of what to expect in up-front costs— initially a negative return and slow growth, gradually increasing in rate of return and size of the benefit. Depending on company strategy, balance the up-front costs, probability, size, and timing of the benefits to prioritize the projects to implement.

Once the initial meetings are complete, make it each team member's responsibility to continuously update the brainstorming activity. Each team member should be relentless in his or her pursuit of improvement and research and should observe and postulate improvements daily to be sure that the company is up to date.

Web Enablement: Other Considerations

The initial brainstorming that we completed focuses mainly on ways to create value from existing resources—either by reducing cost or improving efficiency. Many other benefits are available to e-business, some of which are listed in the following sections. Many of these examples concentrate on the revenue side of the business, but consider activities that go well beyond selling today's products over the Web. It is not only that which we now have, but what we may have if we change to e-business. Consider collaborating with outside experts in each functional area to gain the value of e-business.

Business Segments

Reexamine the business segments in which we now operate to identify the critical success factors and determine whether these characteristics can be used in other businesses. The Web provides us an opportunity to *bridge historical barriers to entry and launch our business to new segments.* In 2001, Pitney Bowes, a secure mail monitoring system developer, received concerned calls from many of its customers about the need for equipment that *protected employees against biological threats*—basically a product line extension. The company had no such equipment in the development pipeline but knew that they must respond to their customers' inquiries. "The company decided that the only way it could respond fast and effectively to the market's sudden shift

Exhibit 4.4

Brainstorming Summary—Opportunity Analysis

(Millions $)

Function	$ Expenses Direct Indirect	Capital	Personnel Resources In-house Outsourced Total	Sales Profits Capital Description	Notes
Primary					
Inbound Logistics					
Operations					
Outbound Logistics					
Marketing & Sales					
Service					
Secondary					
Firm Infrastructure					
Human Resource Management					
Technology Development					
Procurement					
Inbound Material Handling					
Inbound Inspection					
Inbound Transportation					
Total					

Header groupings: Resources (Capital, Personnel Resources), Results (Sales, Profits, Capital Description)

Note: This worksheet and similar worksheets should be prepared for each department, location, or business segment in the company. When completed, you may find that certain functions are performed by departments other than in the particular functional area. For example, it is not unusual to find that procurement—ordering is performed in most departments, even if only for items limited to office supplies, small equipment items, and so forth.

Totals on the master company worksheet should equal the total company investments—approximately. Precision is not as important as efficiently completing the analysis.

Function Note: ( ) is cost.	$ Expenses		Potential Changes	Personnel Resources			Results				Notes
	Direct	Indirect	Capital	In-house	Outsourced	Total	Sales	Profits	Capital	Description	
Primary											
Inbound Logistics	(0.1)	0.1							1.0		Coordinate cross-docking with UPS, reducing inbound handling, inventory investment, shrinkage, etc.
Operations											
Outbound Logistics											
Marketing & Sales											
Service	(0.2)						1.0	0.7			Manage service workload and scheduled preventive maintenance scheduling. Actively market preventive maintenance using service bulletins.
Secondary											
Firm Infrastructure											
Human Resource Management	(0.1)	0.3									Shift health benefits administration to national carrier, improving service levels while reducing expenses.
Technology Development											
Procurement											
Inbound Material Handling		0.5									
Inbound Inspection											
Inbound Transportation											
Total											

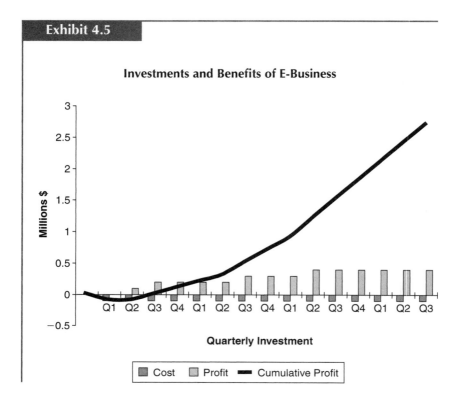

Exhibit 4.5

Investments and Benefits of E-Business

Quarterly Investment

Cost Profit Cumulative Profit

was to look outside for ideas. Within a few weeks, a special team of Pitney Bowes engineers gathered 82 promising concepts from fields as diverse as food handling and military security."[18] Pitney Bowes used an approach called open-market innovation—"an approach that uses tools such as licensing, joint ventures, and strategic alliances to bring the benefits of free trade to the flow of new idea."[19]

Companies can take advantage of similar open-market innovation processes by using innovation exchanges. "It used to take 12 months to 36 months to find a buyer for a promising innovation, and technology transfers generally happened only within an industry. Now innovation exchanges are sprouting up all over the Internet. *TechEx,* for example, grew out of Yale University to become an active site for buyers and sellers of biomedical technology. The site, www.techex.com, has more than 700 companies

---

[18] "Open Market Innovation," by Darrell Rigby and Chris Zook, *Harvard Business Review,* October 2002, pp. 80–89.

[19] "Open Market Innovation," by Darrell Rigby and Chris Zook, *Harvard Business Review,* October 2002, pp. 80–89.

registered as users."[20] In the past, expansion to other business segments may have been prohibitive because of supply chain barriers. However, with Web sales, instant communications, and engineering collaboration, today a company can modify the supply chain, eliminate the distributor network, and deal directly with potential new customers. Challenge the management team to capitalize on these strengths.

Growth Potential

The Web is not just a cost-cutting tool, nor is it a tool to simply increase sales of existing products to a broader geography or trade channel. It is a technology that allows us to change the *rules of business*. As we examine the functional strengths and weaknesses, challenge the executives to identify how we can grow beyond the current boundaries—product, geography, industry, trade channels, customers, and so forth. Each functional area may be a new source of value. Knowledge management and cross-company collaboration have become ideal ways to use Web technology to improve value at a company. "Even in the best of times, it's a battle to convince employees to participate in knowledge management programs. . . . The payoff for getting individuals mobilized around Knowledge Management can be breathtaking. Shell International Exploration and Production attributes more than $200 million in direct costs saved and additional income in 2002 to the use of its SiteScape online collaboration forum. The division has clearly contributed to the success of its parent, Royal Dutch/Shell Group, which was ranked number four on the Fortune Global 500 this year. Royal Dutch/Shell increased its revenue a startling 33 percent from 2001 to 2002."[21]

Profit Potential

The traditional business paradigms may be irrelevant and current business models may be obsolete when you consider the e-business model. Before e-business, an executive team would develop strategies based on historical metrics—asset-to-sales ratios, head count-to-sales ratios, R&D investment intensity, gross profit ratios, sales representatives-to-customer ratios, and G&A as percent-to-sales ratios, E-business will revolutionize your business and make the historical metrics irrelevant. Latex Foam International, the

---

[20] "Open Market Innovation," by Darrell Rigby and Chris Zook, *Harvard Business Review,* October 2002, pp. 80–89.

[21] "Why Three Heads Are Better Than One," by Lauren Gibbons Paul, *CIO Magazine,* December 1, 2003, pp. 95–104.

only U.S. producer making a specialty foam product, lost its only production facility to fire in May 2001. Rather than discontinue operations, the company invested in a modern, digitally controlled factory that allows engineers to manage the facility, "from the mixing of latex and the distribution of liquid rubber into molding beds by mantis-like hanging robots to the heating, cooling, cleaning, and drying of finished foam cores. . . ." The vice president of technology stated, "I can manage [the plant] from my notebook, even at home." Efficiency improved by 30 percent, capacity increased by 50 percent in a smaller space, and facility head count was reduced by about one-third.[22] As a result of rethinking its business, Latex Foam International is more competitive globally. We must also ask, "How can we increase profits with either no increase in investment, or even less investment?"

Business Volatility

How many businesses suffer with a volatile business cycle that disrupts profitability trends and effective resource utilization? The Web capabilities allow companies to smooth the workload by adding instant information to their decision process. When the potential benefits of information are well understood, even the most mundane, low-tech commodity business can benefit. eSuds has combined the instant information capabilities of the Web, an understanding of their service, and their asset investments to create a solution that minimizes their business volatility.

> *eSuds, a division of USA Technologies, re-outfits laundry machines on college campuses with intelligent computer devices. The machines can send repair messages to the operators, when there is a problem or notify them when there is a problem or notify them when maintenance is due. Since a broken machine ceases to generate any money, getting a machine back online quickly is imperative. Additionally, students can view the availability of machines from their dorm rooms using an Internet browser to a dedicated Web site for that laundry facility. The system will also send e-mail notification to the student when the laundry is completed. . . . And best of all, the machines can operate in a complete cashless mode by using student ID. . . .[23]*

eSuds has reduced downtime resulting from maintenance failures, increased uptime by having online equipment utilization access to students, become

---

[22] "The Flexible Factory," by Adam Aston and Michael Arndt, *Business Week,* May 5, 2003.

[23] "Real Time Enterprise: The Ultimate Synergy of Business and Technology," *Business Week,* Special Advertising Section, December 2, 2002.

more user friendly and competitive by having e-mail notification to students, minimized theft, and developed a database that will assist the company in designing and modifying facilities to further improve competitiveness and customer friendliness. Sounds like low-tech has been introduced to hi-tech, doesn't it?

Pace, Flexibility, Adaptability, Creativity

The Web removes or reduces the impact of constraints such as time, adaptability, flexibility, and creativity, because virtually any resource is available to anyone with a computer. For example, historically, in retail, location was a key to profitability. Amazon.com and eBay have changed that paradigm. Amazon.com and eBay have adapted to the new paradigm by developing processes that are secure, consistent, and well controlled. They have also leveraged the processes to expand their product portfolio to many other retail sectors. Better yet, they have expanded beyond products that they themselves ship. Amazon.com has established alliances with other *brick and mortar* sellers to leverage the Amazon process—once again "out-of-the-box" thinking. The company receives a fee for service to process the transaction and will coordinate the completion of the sale and the shipment of the product using its proprietary processes. eBay has actually invested in an "over-the-Web" payment processing technology by purchasing PayPal, which will also generate value as this becomes a standard of Web purchasing.[24] Now the Web is the foundation of PayPal's business at eBay and is also the source of a marketable new service—secure Web payment using PayPal.

Beyond Your Industry

As we consider applications and benefits of "e" implementations, we must look far beyond your industry for solutions. New innovative products may be developed using the Web and the existing base of products. For example, an outsourcing organization may initially envision the existing customer base as the limit for services. Consider the resources in an outsourced customer service organization like Convergys—well-trained, computer-literate, English-speaking personnel who are able to deal effectively with U.S. consumers. The product may initially be "telecom billing information systems," but once the infrastructure is in place, would this same well-controlled process serve other

---

[24] "eBay Completes PayPal Acquisition," eBay Press Release, San Jose, California, October 3, 2002.

outsourcing requirements, such as a medical records facility, credit card tele-marketing, or service organizations?

Once the key elements of the existing products are defined, consider alternatives to expand your product lines and leverage the initial investment. Once the infrastructure is in place, why not?

New Geography

Geography will no longer be restricted to the territory you now serve when you use the Web. Although you may not want a global presence, once you are promoting your product on the Web, you will have a global business. Do not fret—geography can easily be limited by listing areas served on your website, but do not sell yourself short. Where do we operate today? Geography would include not only our physical location but also where you are represented or interact with any of your constituents. Reexamine every functional activity to identify where you perform a function—a storage function, a vendor/procurement function, selling, research, and so forth.

New Collaborations

Does your business plan require that you do everything yourself? Again, consider how Amazon.com has expanded well beyond its original business model of selling books. Amazon.com still sells new books, but now it also sells *used books, clothing, appliances, electronics,* and so forth. Amazon.com has expanded its product lines and leveraged its investment on its core competency—Web-enabled transactions. Amazon.com examined their business processes, identified potential business opportunities, and established business relationships with other vendors who could leverage their systems, business investments, and existing infrastructure. How can we expand beyond our current horizons to capture more value?

What Can the Business Be When Enabled?

Consider Convergys Corp. from Cincinnati, Ohio—one of the largest, most successful outsourcing firms in the world—perhaps by a factor of two compared to their nearest competitor. In the year 2000, their competitors were in the United States—perhaps on the East Coast. Criteria for the customer service organization requirements were fairly simple—access to customer account information and well-trained, English-speaking personnel. During the past few years, the company has hired thousands of employees in India. The key to this shift in sourcing is available, inexpensive, well-trained,

English-speaking personnel with access to customer information. The Internet—global reach with instant access to data files and inexpensive telecommunications capabilities—made this possible. Pre-Internet, expensive access to telephone communications and data prohibited India as an alternative for serving global clients.

A Last Thought

Unfortunately, when we think beyond the horizon we may not have the experience to properly deal with the new environment. You can better develop these brainstorming opportunities in several ways. Professional associations often have thought leaders in specific areas; consider American Production and Inventory Control Society (APICS), Certified Public Accounting organizations, American Marketing Association, Financial Executives International, and so forth. There are also seminars sponsored by these associations, professional consulting organizations (e.g., Accenture, Bain & Company, IBM), organizations that develop and implement solutions (e.g., Oracle, SAP), and companies that have successfully implemented the e-business process. These progressive organizations and companies often will provide insight into many of the features, implementation issues, and value of specific e-business applications. As business leaders, challenge the existing processes.

There may be a downside to some e-business applications. As we develop these e-business alternatives, be careful not to be blindsided by the allure of what appears to be very inexpensive, qualified labor. There are additional costs, time zones to consider, intrinsic knowledge and culture that may be better served by U.S. personnel, and so forth. Be sure that your analysis is balanced and considers the downside potential of each major change anticipated. Based on cost of service, "Web.com CEO Will Pemble decided to 'offshore' his Internet hosting company's customer service. This November, plagued by cultural misunderstandings and lost customers, Pemble brought all of Web.com's call back from India to Brookfield, Conn. In the end Pemble concluded, it was costing his company more to send work to India than to do it in one of the highest-cost states of the Union. Dell made a similar—if much more widely publicized—decision in November, routing calls from some high-end business customers back to Texas from its Indian call center in Bangalore."[25]

---

[25] "Hang-ups in India," *Fortune Magazine,* December 22, 2003, p. 44.

Summary

The e-business analysis is a simple process—assess, plan, and execute based on the available information. The assessment process can be done quite easily using a systematic review of all the functions in your organization. Complete the standardized functional resource templates based on likely benefits, using the executive team's judgment to prioritize by the size of the benefit, the probability of realizing the benefit, and the timing of the benefit. The documented summary of resources and potential benefits will be a solid basis for judging the current status and future performance.

The standardized resource template will also be an excellent foundation for brainstorming to open the gate to a more valuable future. Staff the brainstorming effort with functional experts who have become familiar with or perhaps even trained in selected e-business methods and do not restrict the knowledge to *your industry*—consider how the best companies in the world do the job. Find the best functional expertise and most unique applications on earth—regardless of industry. Remember, eSuds would not have their current solution to competitiveness by looking at the other laundry operators.

Once you have brainstormed, prioritize the opportunities based on your business needs. Many of the applications can be self-funding. Remember the Salesforce.com application, which was implemented in weeks and for several thousand dollars instead of years and several million dollars for a full-blown ERP installation. And remember, *these one-off applications are not just for small companies that cannot afford the multimillion dollar Global ERP application.* Most likely, you will be overwhelmed by the possibilities if you do not prioritize based on your company's strategic needs. Do you need more capacity utilization? Then focus on the functions that will improve utilization, such as expanded sales through the Web.

Thus far we have reviewed the functional structure of an organization, but a more in-depth analysis will focus on activities performed within each function. In the next chapter, we will analyze how a function performs within an organization down through individual direct and indirect activities.

Regardless of what the myriad of software vendors demand, it is not necessary to invest in an entirely new system to engage this "e" world. The smartest people analyze their needs and selectively implement those software enhancements that will benefit them most. In some applications, it is not even necessary to invest in entire ERP packages because many of the critical services are available on an *a la carte* basis. We will have to become more familiar with the software first.

CHAPTER 5

ASSESSMENT—ACTIVITIES AND CONSTITUENTS

Introduction

In the previous chapter, we reviewed the functional areas within a company and identified areas of concentrated spending and opportunity. We also introduced the concept of direct and indirect activities. Direct activities are those that create value for the customer, whereas indirect activities are those that allow the firm to operate smoothly. In this chapter, we will focus on the *activities performed in your firm,* examining examples of direct and indirect activities, and we will also explore analytical methods to better support the e-business investment decisions.

One of the areas of greatest spending is purchasing, and as a result, it is one of the first activities analyzed in an e-business analysis. When you consider the extent of costs that are processed through the purchasing function, and the potential rewards to review purchasing first, early wins through purchasing are an ideal place to generate savings to invest in future Web projects. As in previous chapters, we will concentrate on value to the firm that can be realized through *reducing costs, changing asset investment levels* (e.g., inventory, fixed assets), *changing revenue streams,* or *improving investment utilization* (i.e., smoothing the business cycle).

We will next describe an *activities audit* to identify the activities performed and costs in a functional area to better understand how to change. Ideally, the analysis will identify how to *increase* the amount of direct activity and how to *reduce or eliminate the amount of indirect activity.*

Because changes to expand our e-business activities will affect our *constituents,* we will also assess how the changes affect them. After we understand the impact on constituents, the management team will brainstorm potential changes in activities to improve company value.

As we better understand possible e-business applications, we will compare the applications against the business strategy to prioritize the applications. When we have finished the chapter, we will have reviewed worksheets to assist in the analysis, defined priorities, and gained an understanding of the expected impact on the company and the constituents.

Constituents Defined

Unfortunately, change will not be complete unless all the constituents affected by the changes accept them. During the activity audit, which we will discuss later in the chapter, identify every person or organization that may be affected by the e-business changes. The list should include current and potential customers, vendors, government agencies, employees, retirees, and so forth. Each constituent may be either an ally or an opponent of change to an enabled company. When we review the constituent list, anticipate how they will be affected by minor changes; for major changes, consult with the affected constituents personally. Share the decision and the benefits and make them part of the enablement solution.

For some constituents you will not be able to get feedback before the process changes—such as expanded sales and distribution over the Web to new customers or new vendors through Web open-bidding processes. If you cannot get direct feedback before you open the Web processes, be sure that you have feedback mechanisms on the Web to encourage feedback, monitor response to your changes, and respond to the constituents either personally or globally with changes to your enablement processes. Prepare summaries of correspondence, identify key metrics, review trends, follow up on needed changes, and make an executive responsible for decisions and proper follow-up. The most effective activity audit will consider the impact on constituents throughout the audit.

Activities Defined

Activities can be either direct or indirect. Direct activities create value for the ultimate customer, whereas indirect activities allow the organization to perform the direct activities. Initially, you might expect that direct activities would be concentrated in primary functions and that indirect activities would be concentrated in support functions. Unfortunately, it is not that simple within most companies because direct activities can be performed in virtually any functional area, whereas indirect activities may be performed in primary functions. Indirect activities, such as the ordering of supplies, time reporting, internal project management, and management of internal budgets, are activities that will be performed in a sales operation or inbound logistics, and most likely in all primary functions. Also, direct activities may be performed deep within a support function. The information technology (IT) specialist who designs and manages the Web page for your online catalog is a direct activity within a support function. The contract administrator in the legal department who manages pricing and delivery terms for your key clients is another example of a direct activity managed in the support function.

We will review activities in several ways. The first level of review will separate purchasing from all other activities because companies usually realize immediate benefits from e-business. All other activities will then be examined by first considering a core of indirect activities (e.g., budgeting, planning, training, internal reporting), often performed by all functions. Once these core indirect activities have been discussed, we will focus on direct and other indirect activities often performed in functional areas.

Purchasing Activity

We will review purchasing first because this will most likely provide immediate savings that will be quick and easy to implement. Studies by the Aberdeen Group have shown that "non-production materials like office supplies, computer equipment and maintenance, repair and operating provisions (MRO) . . . can account for 30% to 60% of a company's total expenditures yet they remain poorly controlled and costly to process at most organizations."[26]

Studies have also noted that off-contract buying is more prevalent for services than for direct or indirect products, and service supplier networks are huge, averaging nearly 75 suppliers per purchasing employee—more than double the number of suppliers per buyer of direct goods.[27] As a result of its size, purchasing is generally one of the fastest payback areas using the Web, and not simply because a company uses online bidding processes. Large companies installed enterprise resource planning (ERP) systems to capture this value, but it is not only major corporations that can save through the Web.[28] Hosted e-procurement solutions, or applications systems providers (ASPs)—those that do not require purchase of expensive mainframe computers and fully integrated ERP systems—are now also available to the small to mid-sized users, with low up-front costs, quick implementation time, and minimal routine operating costs to maintain the system. Using a purchasing ASP/ERP system, a company can better control off-contract buying and reduce the

26 "e-Procurement: Finally Ready for Prime Time," Market Viewpoint, by The Aberdeen Group, Volume 14, Number 2, March 21, 2001, p. 1.

27 CFO.com; "A Hire Power: Services E-Procurement Is Quietly Gaining Ground, Helping Companies Control an Expense That Often Escapes Scrutiny," by Anne Stuart, *CFO-IT Magazine,* March 18, 2003.

28 "e-Procurement: Finally Ready for Prime Time," Market Viewpoint, by The Aberdeen Group Volume 14, Number 2, March 21, 2001, p. 1.

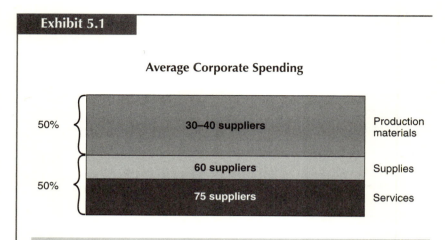

Exhibit 5.1

Average Corporate Spending

Survey of 115 large companies coordinated by the Center for Advanced Purchasing Studies. Adapted from "A Hire Power; Services E-procurement Is Quietly Gaining Ground, Helping Companies Control an Expense That Often Escapes Scrutiny," by Anne Stuart, CFO IT, CFO.com, March 18, 2003.

number of approved suppliers, ultimately reducing administrative costs and purchase costs. Aberdeen Group research indicates that e-procurement deployments of the ASP, when compared with fully integrated ERP systems, reduce deployment time by 23 percent, reduce implementation cost by 60 percent, and reduce overall ongoing operating cost by 40 percent. To realize these benefits, we must more thoroughly understand our business.

Indirect activities, such as sending specifications, reviewing past vendor performance, monitoring shipments, and so forth, can be completed automatically through a properly designed Web application. Services are now available on the Web to expedite purchasing and help maintain consistent, high-quality service. In addition, certain vendors, such as Dell, Staples, and OfficeMax, prefer to sell over the Web because their total costs to manage transactions are minimized. Using the Web, vendors improve inventory logistics and improve control over customer pricing and discount structures, all within the customer-approved purchasing guidelines, which eliminates rogue purchases (e.g., a secretary who ordered a computer for her home use) and ensures predictable service levels.

Benefits that will result from well-defined purchasing enablement include the following:

• Lower administrative costs as a result of reduced clerical work
• Faster procurement cycle time

- Improved negotiating leverage with suppliers as a result of concentrated purchasing
- Fewer suppliers to manage
- Reduced off-schedule buying
- Potential expanded sourcing opportunities with more solutions to purchasing needs
- Reduced logistics cost through online shipping negotiation and so forth

In a 2000 survey, the Aberdeen Group identified the following savings:

	Manually Processed	**E-Business Processed**
Cost per purchase	$121	$33
Cycle time to process	9.7 days	2.5 days[29]

Analyze your current environment, establish performance standards, and quantify potential benefits that will result from enablement alternatives to realize these savings.

Purchasing Analysis

You must first understand the current spending by category, individual vendor, and products purchased and current procurement processes. As you develop the company profile in each of these areas, challenge each element of current activity for change and benefits. A quick example of a product summary follows:

Purchases	Millions $
Electric motors	7.0
Steel	4.0
Reduction gears	2.7
Circuit boards	2.4
Bearings	1.0
Packaging board	0.6

Using a high-low list by commodity, you can identify the commodities that may result with the largest potential savings. However, look beyond the numbers to identify other areas of potential savings—commodity products such as packaging boards may yield significant savings when opened to

---

29 "eProcurement: Finally Ready for Prime Time," Market Viewpoint, by The Aberdeen Group, Volume 14, Number 2, March 21 2001, p. 1.

competitive bidding. Use both a qualitative and quantitative review to identify potential savings for a better analysis.

In a vendor list of summarized purchases, you may also find that you have multiple vendors that provide the same products. Let's examine such a list:

Vendors	Products	Value (Millions $)
Emerson Electric	Electric motors	6.4
Hickman Electric	Electric motors	0.5
Mitsubishi Electric	Electric motors	4.2
Johnson Motors	Electric motors	1.0
Staples	Office supplies	0.7
OfficeMax	Office supplies	0.7
Quill	Office supplies	1.0

A review by vendor will identify multiple vendors for similar products, which may dilute buying power because larger customers often receive volume discounts. As we examine each of these summaries, remember it is not just a question of "How do we get a product cheaper?" but rather "How can we work with these vendors to create more value for our firm?"

Another look at the qualitative aspects of purchasing may show that an electric motor vendor is local, compared to another vendor located 1,000 miles away, but selling identical motors for 1 percent less. How do you compare these values to the firm? The best answer may be that more frequent delivery from the nearby vendor will reduce inventory levels and reduce freight costs. Will we realize higher volume discounts by concentrating purchases? Do not make a common mistake by ordering over the Web based on product cost alone because many variables create company value.

The initial purchasing survey identifying vendor and product spending should be completed in several weeks; do not postpone the overall analysis until every facet of your purchasing is analyzed.

Nonpurchasing Activities—Activity Audit

We should understand where and how we spend our time and money today to effectively prioritize enablement activities in a company. In the previous chapter, we reviewed financial summaries that identified the functional expenses; now we will examine activities and their costs within those functions. In each analysis, we are searching for value, not just cost reduction. Although value can mean cost reduction, it can also mean changes in activities that reduce asset investments, increase leverage, broaden markets, and enhance the quality of revenue through pricing management, load management, and so forth. Prioritization factors such as position in the business life cycle, market and profitability growth potential, and the competitive environment will be the criteria used to evaluate the e-business. We will analyze the activities using several steps.

First, identify whether the company is *centralized* or *decentralized* so that you prioritize the activities and focus resources. Centralized companies often concentrate the support functions and the indirect activities in headquarters' shared-services departments, such as accounting, IT, human resources, legal, and so forth. Centralized companies may also concentrate direct activities for the primary functions in a headquarters' department, such as direct selling, marketing, research and development (R&D), and so on. If the company is centralized, we will first focus on total activity costs in functional areas as a simple way to quantify potential enablement benefits based on costs; we will then consider potential opportunities by changing the activities performed. This analysis could actually result with a change of company structure from centralized to a more decentralized company. Decentralized companies often consist of autonomous business units including all or many of the functions and activities required to operate a business as a business unit. If the company is decentralized, prioritize the initial activity review on total cost by *business unit* and then consider potential value opportunity by changing the activities performed. In decentralized companies, we should also examine the company-wide opportunity for centralization as we examine all primary and support functions and direct and indirect activities. If the survey is completed in a decentralized environment, summarize activity cost within divisions to calculate a total activity cost for the company.

Direct and/or indirect activities within the functional areas can be summarized using one of several activity audit methods, such as informed estimates, group consensus, or survey techniques. Once costs and activities are identified, challenge the need for the activity and the process used for the activity value-added improvements considering cost and other value improving changes.

After you determine whether you are a centralized or decentralized organization, identify the types of activities performed, classify them as direct or indirect, and whenever possible, identify the major financial impact associated with the operations. Three methods used to summarize activities and potential benefits include *top-down estimates, group meetings,* and *actual surveys and studies.* Selection of the best method depends on company structure, personnel competence, personalities, and so forth, so select the method that fits your situation best.

Top-down estimates use the department management's judgment to identify activities, costs, and potential opportunity if activities are changed. First, list all activities, identifying them as direct or indirect, and then estimate the resources required to complete the activity, the assets and liabilities associated with the activity, and the constituents affected by the activity. In a typical department, this should require no more than one-half to a full day.

Brief *group meetings* composed of employees within the function can be used to identify activities performed within that function or department. The meetings should require only a few hours, and attendees will define activities at a high level, classify activities as direct or indirect, and identify associated costs and major assets or liabilities. Because it is a group meeting, it is best to gain consensus about the financial investments and the implications of changes to the activity spending.

Activity surveys and time studies can be completed to identify major activities that are performed within departments and the amount of resources required to perform the tasks. Informed estimates are the best way to complete surveys and to try to avoid precision that may be unnecessary and time-consuming. People who actually perform the work should summarize activities based on *typical work routines* and should also include *nonroutine work* so that we have a complete picture of the function.

Let's look at a functional area to explore in depth how a function is managed.

Exhibit 5.2 includes a profit and loss (P&L) statement of the selling department, which we will examine at several *levels:*

- *Level One* is a traditional P&L in a summarized format. Broadly defined functional spending categories such as selling, marketing, and R&D are often used to manage the day-to-day P&L. Quite often, secondary functions are grouped under administrative headings and include finance, treasury, legal, human resources, and so forth. We have included balance sheet sections in the analysis because the activities may affect the balance sheet accounts. It may also be worthwhile to summarize personnel investments—number of people by type— executive, manager, individual contributor—on the *Level One* and subsequent analyses. It is a judgment call whether you need such detail; you decide if it makes sense.
- *Level Two* represents the natural expense categories—payroll, fringe benefits, and so forth—used to initially record expenses. As you review these expenses, think about what the spending represents—not

Exhibit 5.2

Analysis Levels

Level One		Level Two		Level Three		Level Four	
						Direct	Indirect
Sales	*Millions $* 100.0						
Cost of Sales	50.0						
Gross Profit	50.0						
SG&A							
Selling	**15.0**	Payroll	7.0	Admin—Planning	1.0		1.0
Marketing	6.0	Fringe Benefits	2.0	Admin—Proj Mgmt	1.0		1.0
R&D	5.0	Travel	1.0	Customer Service	1.0	1.0	
Finance	2.5	Consulting	2.0	Direct Selling	6.0	6.0	
Legal	0.5	Supplies	2.0	Sales Travel Time	1.5	1.5	
All Other	3.0	Data Systems	0.5	Sales Travel Expense	1.5	1.5	
Total	32.0	Other	0.5	Customer Research	1.5	1.0	0.5
		Total	**15.0**	Other	1.5	0.5	1.0
PBT	18.0			**Total**	**15.0**	**11.5**	**3.5**

The objective is to analyze through the four levels, then eliminate nonvalue activities and reduce indirect activities using the Web or convert to direct using the Web.

just the dollar amounts—because hidden activities may be buried in the costs. For example, consulting costs may include the direct charges of the *consultants* as well as *travel costs.* But within the consultants' direct hourly charges, costs may include *travel time, training time, market research, surveys, interviews,* and *market analysis*—each of which may have different direct or indirect activity classification. Consultants may also include outsourced activities, such as payroll processing, which are essential to manage the business but somehow have become less visible to management.

- *Level Three* analysis identifies the particular activities performed by the function and is the key to understanding the costs and type of activities completed. Level Three activities are quite descriptive of the actual activities performed and could include a description as simple as budgeting, invoicing, managing advertising purchases, training, direct selling, product development/design, and so forth. The analysis should be completed quickly and with reasonable detail so that the executives understand the activities actually performed within a function.

- *Level Four* represents the final distribution of costs to direct and indirect categories. As these costs are summarized in the categories, think about why the company performs the activity. Major cost concentrations should be analyzed further to identify alternatives to today's process. When you finally see how you spend money, you may choose to manage the company differently.

Once we have identified where we spend our resources, we should brainstorm alternatives to the current activities considering the Web advantages in communication, research and transaction processing, and the company's business strategy. Time and cost to implement changes and probable benefits are important to select activities to enable. For example, sales over the Web focusing on available capacity in specific areas such as manufacturing and service may increase sales immediately, whereas establishing a Web training process will provide long-term strategic selling benefits. Promoting certain products or services over the Web may also increase sales immediately.

Understand Strategy

Select Web applications to achieve strategic goals and avoid Web-enablement projects that are "nice to have" but not essential. "Nice-to-haves" are distracting and will dilute your resources. If the company has a growth strategy or a cost-cutting and containment strategy, the Web activities implemented will vary. If revenues are to be built organically, the result will be different than if you will be growing through acquisition or licensing. Some examples of differing strategies and Web alternatives that may be affected are discussed in the following sections.

Acquisition

If you intend to expand through acquisition, will you be acquiring entire companies, divisions, or simply products? If you will be acquiring products, will the products be within the existing products' families or types? For example, service revenue may be a family of products that you have, and expansion may require retraining of the sales and service personnel. Also, if acquired products are new families, the Web can be used to promote the products to existing and new customers and to open new trade channels.

If entire divisions or companies are acquired, determine how their products/services will integrate into your product lines. If you acquire market segments or geographic coverage, how will enablement benefit these expansions? Enablement benefits may be significant, and they may then be critical success factors in the acquisition. When you identify these benefits, you should also be wary of increased implementation risks, additional costs, resource requirements, timelines, and the probability of success. Market expansion may be one of the most challenging in an acquisition, and Web enablement may be an ideal method to simplify the integration of the companies.

Asset Intensity

Web enablement will change the amount of assets required for operations because asset utilization and business pace will improve. As companies become enabled, working capital requirements will decline and cash flow will improve because the business pace accelerates. Historically, computers had a pipeline of products that reached nearly 6 months' cycle time from manufacture to customer. Dell reduced the cycle time to less than 10 days and also reduced inventory levels, fixed asset requirements (less manufacturing and warehouse space required), and accounts receivable because many shipments were fully paid when shipped.

Other Opportunities

Let's examine how enablement will improve performance within primary and support functions. The list is not all-inclusive but rather an introduction to some successful applications already used by many companies—maybe your competitors. We will review activities within the firm, identify the added value of each activity, and then improve the process, using available Web technology and processes. As we examine the direct and indirect activities, we should first challenge how we can completely eliminate the activity; if that is not feasible, we should consider how we can use the Web to improve speed, benefit the constituent, reduce investment levels, and improve asset/liability utilization through reduced cycle time, load balancing, and so forth. We will first examine recurring indirect activities, which can often benefit from e-business.

Recurring Indirect

Indirect activities, such as budgeting, financial planning, scheduling, approving and submitting bills for payment, training employees, meeting with vendors, coordinating travel, ordering supplies, and so forth, can be reviewed for the total company or individual business unit, because a changed process should affect all areas. Each of these activities can be improved using the Web. Ideally, we should improve these indirect activities and either adapt them to the Web or completely eliminate them. As we review the indirect activities, think about how telecommuting can be used not only to reduce costs but also to improve productivity, create access to resources otherwise unavailable, and reduce space requirements. Based on the International Telework Association & Council definition of *teleworker* as an employee who works at home, at a client's office, in a satellite office or telework center, or on the road at least 1 day per month, there are 23.5 million teleworkers in the United States. "Four companies that employ large numbers of teleworkers—Cigna, Hewlett-Packard, AT&T, and Sun Microsystems—report both jumps in productivity and savings on office space. In the current fiscal year, Sun reported a $71 million reduction in, or avoidance of, office-space expense due to teleworking, according to Eric Richert, vice president of the company's iWork Solutions Group, in Newark, California. At AT&T, telework director Joseph Roitz reports that the extra hour of work gained each day by telecommuters last year translated into a $148 million operational benefit. And Cigna's 6,000 'E-Workers' delivered 4-12 percent more output than office workers doing similar work, not to mention the $3,000 per employee the company saved on reduced office space ..."[30] Do not cut costs, but improve value!

---

[30] "Your Place or Mine?" by Doug Bartholomew, *CFO-IT Magazine,* Spring, 2004, pp. 32–38.

Exhibit 5.3

Level 4 Analysis—Develop Opportunities

Level Three	Level Four Direct	Indirect	Notes	Opportunity Analysis
				Implement CRM to better manage A-B-C customers.
				Increase face time with reps by classifying meeting purpose; substitute teleconference for general contact calls, brief information calls. More sales prospecting to new customers on the road. Use the Web, e-mail for routine contact to maintain visibility and relationships.
Admin—Planning	1.0	1.0		
Admin—Proj Mgmt	1.0	1.0		
Customer Service	1.0		A	Consider IP telephony to cut long-distance charges; option is that this will reduce all long-distance costs for the company.
Direct Selling	6.0		B	Expand call center hours to 24 hours per day using telecommuting, mobile technology, and on-call staff.
Sales Travel Time	1.5			
Sales Travel Expense	1.5			
Customer Research	1.5	0.5	C	Establish an FAQ section on the website for 24-hour access to information.
Other	0.5	1.0		
Total	**15.0**	**11.5**	**3.5**	

A = Approx. 25% of all calls are in three main areas: initial system startup, misunderstanding of invoicing, and looking for sales rep.
B = The company has a fleet of cars for sales personnel—face time approx. 40%. We also have $0.5 million call center in use from 8–5 PM EST.
C = Includes about $0.3 million of long-distance charges.

Primary Functions

Inbound logistics includes activities to receive and distribute raw material, components, and parts either to the warehouse for final distribution or to the warehouse for use in the operations function. Direct activities include coordinating inbound transportation, receiving, inspecting/testing products, and organizing products for distribution to the operations process. How can enablement change the activity? Some companies use dynamic scheduling to smooth the flow of goods through inbound logistics to reduce inventory levels, non-value-added activity, and queue time. Standardized receiving documents, being prepared in advance and transmitted over the Web, allow for early review of the information; therefore, when the shipment is received, only final disposition, rather than paperwork review and then disposition, will be completed. When you consider the Web capabilities of real-time information, *inbound logistics* and *outbound logistics* can also be synonymous. Dell does not physically receive some of its merchandise but only cross-docks products at their shipper directly to the customer.

Operations activities include activities to convert raw materials, subcontracted materials, design changes, and labor and machine content into a marketable product for the customer. Direct activities within this function include most activities completed by the direct labor force, as well as some activities completed by indirect labor. Activities performed on the factory floor, in the machine or paint shop, and so forth, including recording transactions, time reporting, and routine communications, can be improved using the Web. It is even possible to eliminate product movement to and from storage areas by producing to fill an order rather than to stock.

Some in-house direct activities may be totally eliminated by outsourcing activities, such as engineering design to be done in China, India, or even Indiana. Through the benefits of real-time communications, you may schedule just-in-time (JIT) deliveries directly to the factory floor, reducing non-value-added goods movement and inventory storage. Ball bearings may be viewed as commodity products—low-margin, slow-moving products that are not very innovative and are available from many countries. The Timken Company, headquartered in Canton, Ohio, decided to challenge the trend to outsource the product to offshore suppliers by using the Web and today's computer-assisted design and manufacturing capabilities to produce in the apparently "high-cost" noncompetitive United States. They invested $150 million in a prototype "bearing plant" in Asheboro, North Carolina, to produce advanced bearings for industrial machinery. The plant is also an incubator to define, test, debug, and roll out advanced technology to production lines at its *76 bearing plants around the globe.* How can they be successful in a high-cost area? A critical success factor to the plant's flexibility is its growing library of digital 3-dimensional models of components, which can be modified and networked to machine tools at the Asheboro facility, *or anywhere in the world where the automated equipment exists.* Gary Endres, Timken's director of order fulfillment says, "Asheboro can go from a work order to a finished part in four hours, down from six to eight weeks in a traditional setup. Down the road, data used to machine a part will also become a market, helping workers track defects, fix them in the field, and plan product revisions. What's more, digital designs from one facility can be zapped in an instant around the world to any other plant."[31]

Outbound logistics includes the activities necessary to select and distribute the products to the customers. These activities include warehouse handling, packaging loading to trucks/mail, and so forth, and eventual shipping to the customers. Real-time transportation pickup can reduce internal handling costs, space requirements, and inventory levels. Real-time freight negotiation will reduce freight costs due to competitive bidding. Web enablement in outbound logistics can also change costs by selecting Web-enabled carriers. For example, FedEx, UPS, Yellow Corp., and other enabled carriers provide online tracking services that eliminate or reduce the time to "expedite" customer orders. Scanning equipment, standardized shipping containers, customer profiles, and shipping conditions reduce or eliminate the indirect activity of preparing unique packing slips, understanding shipping terms, and so forth. In fact, if adequate standards are developed, all shipping activity can be done in advance of the actual shipping time, virtually eliminating the indirect activity at the shipping point, reducing the fulfillment cycle and total outbound logistics activity.

E-business has also helped The North Face better manage its inventory, pricing, and overhead administrative costs. The North Face managed a product line of more than 12,000 SKUs (Stock Keeping Units) with more than 2,000 vendors to sell $238 million of product, while losing $100 million a year because they produced too much inventory and could not match supply to shipments requirements. They implemented Brio software that prepares numerous reports (to improve sales, inventory, and profitability reporting) that are distributed to The North Face decision makers by e-mail. Through improved inventory management, The North Face has reduced

---

31 "The Flexible Factory," by Adam Aston and Michael Arndt, *Business Week,* May 5, 2003, pp. 90–91.

excess inventory by 65 percent, completes 97.5 percent of its orders on time (versus only 90 percent before), and has closed 13 of its 16 outlet stores. Supply chain and operations software is an ideal investment when you consider that, "the median return for operations/production analytics was 277 percent, far more than the median return of 139 percent for financial/business management and 55 percent from CRM applications. . . ."[32]

A fairly successful ASP application is @Road®, which provides real-time tracking and reporting of delivery assets, interactive place-to-place routing, and resource management. The product is available for both small and large companies and, on a "dot.com" basis, is successful and has staying power. The company is now cash flow positive, after initial start-up in 2002.[33]

Marketing and sales direct activities include selling, promoting, advertising, pricing, negotiating, and quoting. Customer resource management (CRM) is a function that we often associate with improved Web utilization; it is used to provide information to the sales and customer service representatives about all points of contact and discussions with the customers. Files contain notes about open opportunities, in-process transactions, recent shipments, backorders, and so forth. Rather than just manage a particular product sale to a customer, use CRM to mine or extract information from data that are stored in the system. By using the database, the sales/marketing team can manage unique promotional programs, smooth a business cycle, more effectively manage pricing and profitability, and improve the critical customer relationships on a real-time basis. CRM can be a multimillion dollar installation in a Fortune 50 company or a one-off installation in a small consumer products company. Salesforce.com is an ASP that provides easy, inexpensive CRM support to businesses of all sizes with a very short lead time. Salesforce.com provides improved real-time information, improved communication, and reduced administration, allowing sales and customer representatives to focus on the direct sales effort rather than internal administrative effort. Salesforce.com assisted Wachovia Corporation, an organization with more than 13,000 associates and $225 billion in assets, in improving their sales force utilization. Wachovia Corporation originally had an in-house, homegrown sales CRM system that had become dysfunctional in both its maintenance and utility to the sales force. Wachovia Corporation implemented Salesforce.com with two of its institutional sales teams in

---

[32] "Everything Must Go," by Russ Banham, *CFO-IT Magazine,* Summer, 2003, pp. 31–37.

[33] "Wee Web Wonders," by David Kirkpatrick, *Fortune Magazine,* March 8, 2004, p. 200.

6 weeks, including customization, mapping the group's unique processes, and training the employees. As a result, sales representatives are saving at least 30 hours a month of administrative time and spending more "face time" with the customers. The representatives have also coordinated with other sales divisions at Wachovia to sell a bundle of products to the customer in a single sales effort, whereas earlier, two separate sales efforts proposals and client contacts were required.[34]

Many of the sales force's activities can be standardized by using real-time communication and templates to minimize the time required. Using a CRM database, sales representatives can multiply their effectiveness by creating standardized, yet personalized, templates to communicate with their customers—depending on variables such as customer type, sales channel, and size or geography of the customer. By using the databases, the representative can convert raw communication time into a more personalized approach to the customer. What else can benefit the sales areas? Quote preparation can be standardized based on specific variables directly linked to customers, reducing development work, exceptions, unapproved terms and conditions, delivery schedules, and so forth.

A *service* technician often services the equipment at the customer site, but with today's technology, machinery can be monitored through the Web, with preventive maintenance scheduled based on performance. Sometimes, the maintenance can even be completed remotely over the Web. You can change the maintenance strategy to build communications into the service to improve customer satisfaction using the Web. Indirect activities such as urgent service bulletins or service manual updates can be available to your customers 24/7 on the Web to improve serviceability. As companies expand to service contracts, contract administration can be simplified using wireless personal digital assistants (PDAs) to price/quote service and manage the accounts. Wireless laptops with digital camera access can assist in problem diagnosis and solutions.

Service scheduling, customer and employee training, preventive maintenance programs, and remote monitoring can all be accomplished using the Web. We can even develop new products using the Web—maintenance contracts and performance monitoring services may be saleable additional products that can be created using the Web, because they are based on information.

---

34 "Wachovia Corporation Forges Strong and Profitable Client Relationships with Help from Salesforce.com," Salesforce.com Case Study.

Support Functions

Although *support functions* are generally indirect and not customer value-added activities, even secondary functions can perform direct activities. Think about how the Web can change the aspects of indirect activities to direct value-added activities.

Quite often, the accounting department is a function that records transactions and catches errors, such as pricing and discount errors. However, if we use the Web in the accounting process, pricing and contract sale terms can be managed interactively from the field using tables, approved pricing and discounts, contract checklists, and controls. Field personnel can create approved quotes without additional approvals if the system is well designed. Progressive Insurance has received awards for its direct-to-consumer processes, which automatically create approved quotes and also compare costs to competitive carriers. They have effectively automated a process that historically has been very personal and sales force intensive. Pricing-optimization software, available from companies such as i2 and Manugistics, allows companies to squeeze profits from customers by projecting the highest price that customers will tolerate before moving to competitive products. During a March 2003 earnings conference call, Stephen Sadove, vice chairman of Saks, discussed some of his company's uses and deployments of price-optimization technology. "We have pilots in Saks Fifth Avenue . . . where we're seeing some substantial margin improvement in our private branding business. . . ."[35]

Contracts, leases, and other legal agreements can be automatically managed for renewals, special features and controls, and legal notifications using simple database management processes. Repetitive contract negotiations can even be simplified by using approved templates that are available online. As sales and business development personnel negotiate with the prospective customers, approved contract guidelines can be accessed for immediate commitment without further intervention or approvals. Approved guidelines will empower the business development and sales representatives and improve customer service.

Human resources management and employee training can often be improved using the Web. Human resources management is generally an indirect function performing indirect activities because there is very little contact with the customer. Activities that are often included within the human resources function include hiring, personnel registrations, performance reviews,

---

[35] "Adding Price Optimization to the CRM Menu," by Erika Morphy, CRM Daily.com, April 18, 2003.

changes in employee status, insurance claims, status changes, and so on. Each of these activities can be completed on the Web, without any additional human intervention, to minimize personnel requirements. Employee training can be completed online to familiarize employees with company policy, procedures, and technical and product training. One of the largest certified public accountant (CPA) firms, Deloitte Touche Tohmatsu, reduced its average training cost per employee by 60 percent from $7,500 to $3,000 between 1999 and 2002 by using more online education.[36] As the world becomes more litigious and the regulatory agencies such as the Occupational Safety and Health Administration (OSHA) and the U.S. Food and Drug Administration (FDA) become more rigid in their requirements, the Web becomes an ideal way for employees, consultants, and vendors to maintain skills required for compliance with good business practices or legal requirements. Often, these programs are administered through the human resources department, who must also manage record keeping.

When the outside world is considered, recruiting done through the human resources department has now become enabled through many ASPs, including sites like Monster.com, which assists candidates and employers in the job search process. Monster.com and dozens of sites like it are automated methods of matching candidate skills and experience with job specifications. In fact, the entire retained and contingent search processes have been irrevocably changed through the use of such sites, which minimize the value of the search firm's proprietary databases while accelerating the search processes using real-time databases. Any potential employee can now access search sites such as Monster.com, but quite often, they can also directly access the "Open Positions" section of a company that is Web enabled and apply directly to the company online. Although this will not work for many of the high-level executive positions, positions for individual contributors, supervisors, and mid-level managers can often be filled using these methods.

Companies such as TALX provide Web enablement through the ASP model for mid- to large-sized companies to perform services such as unemployment claims' handling and analysis, employment and income verifications, electronic pay stubs and cards, direct deposit maintenance, W-4 updates, remote time reporting, and so on, which can all be interfaced with other company-owned or contract services (e.g., ADP, Oracle, Lawson). The services are legally compliant, available 24/7, and paid for on an *a la carte*

---

36 "Online CPE—Getting Easier All the Time," by Robert A. Seay, Holly R. Rudolph, and Margaret N. Boldt, *Journal of Accountancy*, July 2003, pp. 63–66.

basis. Yes, the human resources department can eliminate the drudgery with little fixed cost and be state of the art!

R&D may not historically interact with the customer and outside experts, but this paradigm will change. Because real-time communication and collaboration are Web advantages, companies will find that people who were historically restricted to the back room will begin to interact with outsiders—customers, the sales force, marketing, vendors, and the factory. As the product development cycle shortens in the global environment, companies will find that the communications channels blur and often overlap. Only a foolish company would attempt to limit this communication while their competitors manage the relationships across the company and across the globe with customers and vendors in real time. In the past few years, Procter & Gamble (P&G) has encouraged intracompany and external product development communications, and as a result, new product introductions from external sources have increased from 20 percent in 2000 to about 35 percent in 2004. Product development cycle times at P&G have improved from 3 years to 18 months as a result of collaboration, changes in test marketing, and changes in priorities.[37]

Technology exchanges, such as http://www.techex.com, offer collaborative services to more than 700 companies and are a successful approach to open market innovation. Extending your research sources to the open market will reduce development cycle time and most likely total cost of innovation. Air Products has extended its capacity for innovation by coordinating its collaborative research projects through a central office. "Less than 10% of the company's R&D is conducted by outside partners, but those projects have disproportionate benefits: Each collaboration saves an average of two years of internal effort. Most external projects save the company hundreds of thousands of dollars in net research costs. And the average external research project generates tens of million in potential revenues and millions in potential profits."[38]

Products sold can be expanded to include R&D services or information sold to others, as well as the development of products for your company. If you invent and patent an idea that is not useful to your company, is it valuable to others? Is it marketable on the Web, converting inventoried knowledge to realized value? Consider the impact of immediately accessible information available on university and corporate databases all over the world. In

---

[37] "P&G: Teaching an Old Dog New Tricks," by Patricia Sellers, *Fortune Magazine,* May 31, 2004, pp. 166–180.

[38] "Open-Market Innovation," by Darrell Rigby and Chris Zook, *Harvard Business Review,* October 2002, pp. 80–89.

a recent Harvard Business review, the authors applauded the use of a new technique called "open innovation for global product development."[39] The Web enables immediate communication and collaboration around the globe to share and further develop new technology uses. Automotive companies such as Mercedes-Benz have used the Web to improve overall product development across the globe. Other companies such as The Hackett Group have developed new *information products* from existing internal databases developed as byproducts of their main consulting business. Research consists of their raw data packaged into more easily interpreted information that can be displayed using various selection factors, such as demographics, geography, industry segments, and so on.

The Web has enabled remote software development in countries such as India. During 2003–2004, India has become a leader in software development because of the availability of well-trained, English-speaking IT personnel.

Prioritize by Value to the Firm

As we examine these activities, the number of opportunities could overwhelm us without our implementing any of them. Prioritize the activities for implementation by using both opportunity and cost as screens. To estimate the potential project benefits, we will first evaluate the activities in a brainstorming session attended by executives from all functional areas. This brainstorming prioritization will be completed simultaneously with the functional discussion in the 2- to 3-day session outlined in an earlier chapter using the following two steps.

First estimate the value of the activity considering the timing and probability to complete and the possible variability on the results achieved. Benefits that are achieved years from now are less valuable than those that occur sooner, and benefits with a high degree of variability are riskier investments. Exhibit 5.4 shows an example of how to rank various projects considering costs, benefits, and probabilities. A relatively unlikely $5 million P&L benefit 3 years from now does not compare in priority to $500,000 P&L benefit in 12 months. If you have a series of very successful small Web projects in the near term, you will realize not only financial benefits but also improved morale by improving the way you manage the company. Success is a very motivational result of early wins. The summary may also include "soft" evaluations that describe competitive advantages of Web enablement. Once

---

[39] "A Better Way to Innovate," by Henry W. Chesbrough, *Harvard Business Review,* July 2003, pp. 12–13.

Exhibit 5.4

Business Priority Worksheet

Index	Description Project	Benefit	Strategic Linkage	Time to Implement (Months)	Resources	Benefits: Cost $ (Millions $)	Benefits: P&L (Millions $)	Benefits: Balance Sheet (Millions $)	Probability Percentage	Payback (Millions $)
1	Collaborate with Xiang-Chu on Project X-Ray	Digital X-ray launch moved up by 1 year	Accelerate new product development	24	1 Web consultant; 3 internal IT managers	1.0	10.0	—	Low	3.0
2	Launch online service manuals	Competitive advantage over #1	Build customer relationships	3	1 internal IT manager	0.1	—	—	High	—
3	Install CRM for capital sales force	Reduce travel by 5%, expand sales to new geography	Expand market penetration	4	External consultants + 1 internal IT manager	0.1	5.0	—	Medium	3.0

Notes: The X-ray project has a relatively low probability because of the implementation time of 24 months and the likely requirement for FDA approval. The project will also require a large proportion of our internal IT resources.

Online service manuals will give us a competitive edge over Blitzz Medical, who relies only on U.S. mail to release service bulletins.

CRM is one of the greatest advantages that we can gain. Better resource management will allow for broader market penetration and also possible entry into new trade channels.

again, executive judgment is necessary when you evaluate the projects. Rank the results based on their fit with the company strategy.

Exhibit 5.4 is an example of a worksheet that summarizes some Web-enablement activities.

If the benefits cannot be easily estimated, highlight the activities for further analysis. When you have finished the summary of direct and indirect activities, all company costs should be summarized. The size, probability, and timing of the benefits should be used to prioritize the activities for change.

Summary

In this chapter, we reviewed activities performed throughout the functions within the organization. We discussed ways to identify the business constituents and specific methods to summarize how we invest in our company. Informed estimates by management, group discussion, and detailed surveys will provide the essential insight into how we invest, with whom we deal on a routine basis, and the benefits of changing to a more Web-enabled business process. Examples of business summaries and the quantitative and qualitative aspects of the analysis were covered in several exhibits. One key to successful Web enablement is to be sure that all the tactics are fully integrated with the strategic framework.

Once we have these facts to make decisions, we should review the transition timelines, implementation risks, resources available, and the probability of success. Each of these decision elements is inherently risky because we are discussing the unknown future. Executive judgment considering both the tangible and intangible elements of enablement is essential to make the transition.

We have now covered all the basics to develop a business strategy that will embrace Web enablement. The examples that describe our current business, constituents, and traditional business process have been discussed in this chapter and the earlier ones.

The next chapter will focus on strategy—how to develop and implement it. The e-business strategy will be based on the long-term impact of e-business on the company processes and functions (including scope and geography), the company valuation, and the impact on the company constituents. E-business removes all boundaries and enables companies to improve business process and increase the value added.

CHAPTER 6

DEVELOPING A STRATEGY

Introduction

During the past few chapters, we have examined many of the tactical management issues. In this chapter, we will review strategy alternatives developed using our new knowledge of the Web. The Web will increase the benefit of the current strategy because e-business will improve competitiveness. We will review the macro effects of e-business that affect every company, and then we will examine two strategy methodologies often used by companies for planning. Although we concentrate on these two, any strategic planning process can be modified to reflect the Web macro effects. Last, we will examine business cost drivers and the impact of the Web. Again, the individual drivers may vary, but macro factors will affect the cost structure of any business.

There are five macro factors that affect how companies compete in the future.

1. *Pace:* Business pace reflects not only the speed at which issues arise but also the cycle time to resolve them. We will see that enablement is essential to succeed in the new fast-paced global economy.

2. *Architecture:* An open architecture or open-mindedness will encourage unsolicited ideas and improvements from within or outside the company from all constituents. The open architecture requires that executives be highly skilled and confident of their ability to accept critical feedback from all constituents.

3. *Globalization:* Globalization changes our view of the world to a view beyond the traditional visible horizon. The impact of globalization ensures that constituents will not be familiar to management, and management must adapt to a broader market.

4. *Education and employee training:* Learning capabilities and employee training must be expanded to respond to the increased global technical demands and the open and unrestricted architecture.

5. *Structure:* Organization structure must be flatter and responsibilities broadened to match the business pace, open architecture, and globalization. Structure and employee empowerment must be adapted to the new economy to be successful.

We will review two well-regarded strategic planning methods as examples of today's strategy processes—the first developed by The Boston Consulting Group and the next by Michael Porter—to show how companies can adapt to the Web. These strategic processes focus either on the current/ expected business marketplace position (cash cow, star, dogs, or [?]) or on the strategy of a technology leader versus cost leader. Either of these strategic methods can be Web enabled, as can any other strategic planning process.

We will understand how Web processes can be adapted to the existing strategic planning process, regardless of the strategic paradigm used. We will also analyze the impact of the new e-business paradigm on the cost drivers because the drivers will change through enablement. By the end of this chapter, you will have a framework to adapt the Web enablement strategies to your existing strategic planning processes, assess the organization as it relates to macro factors, and also understand the impact of the Web on your business drivers. Adapting the existing strategy to an e-business will expand your outlook to new constituents, flatten and empower your organization structure, focus on training and the skills required to be successful, and accelerate the pace at which you manage. Enabled companies will lead the competition by accelerating business cycle times and compressing to a flatter, more responsive organization, staffed with learning enabled personnel who can excel in the new competitive environment.

Macro Effects of E-Business on Strategy

During the 1990s, business process cycles accelerated compared with earlier decades and broader global exposure required that companies change to be successful. Geopolitical forces developed new markets as suppliers and customers in the Far East and Eastern Europe became more competitive and integrated into the new global economy.

Exhibit 6.1 identifies the five macro effects of e-business that should be integrated into any strategic planning process. These factors will affect almost every business, anywhere in the world, although the impact will vary depending on the industry and competitive conditions. As you prepare your strategic plan, assess your capabilities for each of these factors compared with the industry best and overall best global practices. Your strategic plan should identify the most significant factors, and when necessary, you should develop a plan to implement improvements. A brief discussion of each macro effect of e-business follows.

Exhibit 6.1

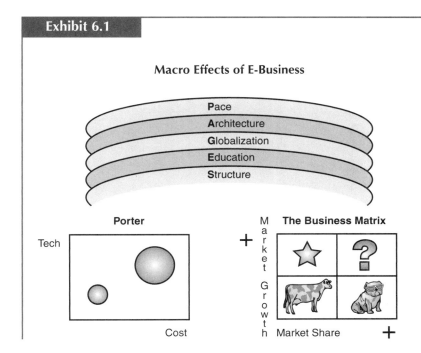

Macro Effects of E-Business

Pace
Architecture
Globalization
Education
Structure

Porter

Tech

Cost

The Business Matrix

Market Growth

Market Share

Pace/Timing

Today, major world events happen *quickly* and *unpredictably* and are known instantly around the globe. When Iraq invaded Kuwait in the early 1990s, CNN broadcast the information globally, the cost of oil futures changed immediately, and gas prices at the pump reached new highs within days. In 1997, NASA's website attracted 47 million views/visitors to view Mars within 4 days of the *Sojourner's* landing on the planet. What would have happened if life were observed?[40]

Cycle time for events is quicker than ever. It took decades of research to identify DNA and, in a concerted effort, only 2 to 3 years to identify all the components of the human genome. Not only do the events that occur all over the globe affect us, but also activities process in shorter, more compressed cycles.

As we consider more than 200 countries, more than 5 billion people, and millions of small and large businesses, daily events will somehow affect your business—even if only remotely. If that is true, then why do we

---

[40] "Business @ the Speed of Thought," by Bill Gates, Warner Books, 1999, New York, p. 116.

attempt to create 3- to 5-year strategic plans and rely on questionable and outdated assumptions? In an enabled world, new competitors or scientific developments arise from other countries without warning. Long-range plans are, at best, scenarios from which financial results may be achieved if a company is flexible and adapts to ever-changing conditions. As you prepare your strategic plan, accelerate into the future. *The strategic planning time frame should reflect faster business cycles, perhaps a shorter time horizon, and a concerted effort to accelerate critical business processes in your organization.* Do not attempt to change all of them, but change the critical few that will make your company more successful. As an example, select the most significant three activities in your business and compare the cycle time to the best in the world—in any business. If you do not compare favorably against the *best,* define how you can change the activity in your strategy. Keep your strategic planning cycle brief and periodically refreshed to reflect major changes. Assume that the pace of change affecting your business will accelerate, and if you are planning effectively, you will lead your industry cost or technology innovation.

Architecture—Open to the World

An open architecture company is an organization trained to cultivate sources and encourage, accept, and interpret information and ideas from all constituents. Topical areas are unlimited and can include very focused information about products, services, and processes or broad areas such as attitudes or cultures. Message boards and anonymous feedback on a website may be the best examples of free unbiased communications. With the Web's reach, a company can collaborate with universities, government agencies, other industries, competitors, and so forth, to improve processes and products. An open architecture will require an extremely well-trained, confident organization that can develop policies and procedures to successfully interpret a continuous flow of information and execute decisions based on the information. This learning organization will be in the best competitive position in the industry in the world. If your competitor has such an organization, how long can you compete if you do not do the same?

Globalization

Thirty years ago, the typical office migrated from carbon paper to the electrostatic copier, improving communication and efficiency in the organization by distributing information quickly and easily to a broader audience.

The fax machine improved the pace and breadth of communication by transmitting information across the globe without days of delay. In the 1990s, the Web and e-mail allowed instant communication, which once again accelerated the pace of business. Access to data and instant two-way communication has changed progressive companies.

Globalization has changed the personal and legal interactions of companies. Business constituents with whom we interact daily are no longer close friends or personal acquaintances, but possibly just names on an e-mail. We may no longer know with whom we are corresponding (e.g., credentials, credibility, country, business) or from where the next communication will originate. The social, economic, and legal environments and varied backgrounds of personnel with whom we deal on the Web no longer allow us to interact as in the past with neighboring constituents in the United States. Globalization in today's Web-enabled world requires a different business approach not only because cultures vary but also because there are fewer personal relationships. A decade ago, Mexico enjoyed a privileged relationship with the United States through the North American Free Trade Agreement (NAFTA). Electronics, textiles, furniture, toys, and footwear manufacturing deserted U.S. sites in favor of Mexican sources years ago. During the past few years, those industries have now deserted Mexico in favor of China, where an assembly-line worker earns $0.50 to $0.80 per hour compared to $2.50 to $3.50 per hour in Guadalajara.[41]

Foreign laws and regulations that were never before encountered must now be properly administered. What is the competitive impact of selling a medical device over the Web? If a French manufacturer with a device approved by the European Union (EU) wanted to sell the product in the United States, supposedly they must comply with U.S. Food and Drug Administration (FDA) regulations. In today's environment, however, the French company could promote and sell the product on the Web and perhaps not comply with the U.S. regulations. How does that change a U.S. company's ability to compete in the marketplace? If a U.S. company wants to sell a product in France, what is required? To be effective, you may want to create an entirely new organization to deal with the complexities of global business. You may interact with a new classification of constituents such as international brokers, foreign attorneys, certified public accountants (CPAs), and regulatory specialists as a result of globalization.

---

[41] "Wasting Away: Despite SARS, Mexico Is Still Losing Export Ground to China," by Geri Smith, *Business Week,* June 2, 2003, pp. 42–43.

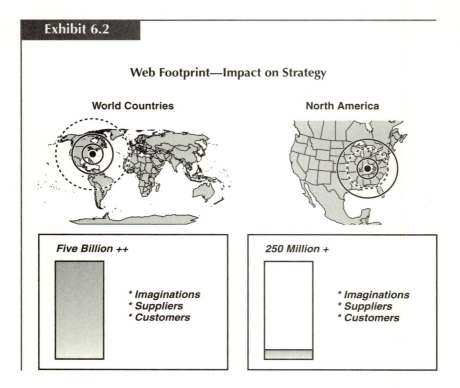

Exhibit 6.2

Web Footprint—Impact on Strategy

World Countries

North America

Five Billion ++

* Imaginations
* Suppliers
* Customers

250 Million +

* Imaginations
* Suppliers
* Customers

If you do not prioritize business programs to manage globalization, constituents from around the globe will distract and disorient you in relation to your strategy. Be selective as to how you open your business to the globe in both outbound and inbound activity.

Education

As we have seen, pace, architecture, and globalization demand an educated and further trainable workforce to be successful. The education and training may be technical (e.g., the laws of the EU, Spanish/French language, or country regulatory standards) or soft skills (e.g., business etiquette in Japan, knowledge of rugby, or the history of 20th-century Poland). These skills cannot be static because more than 200 countries may interact with your business and you may have to deal with future unforeseen relationships. As you plan the strategy, assess the business gaps in the soft and hard skills needed to achieve the strategy and determine how to resolve the gaps. The specific education gaps need not be filled exclusively by employees; they can be filled by consultants, brokers, or other specialists in both technical and soft-skill areas.

Structure

Multilayered organizations will not be successful in the new enabled environment because they cannot function in such a fast-paced, open, global environment. The organization structure should be compressed to allow for fast, effective assessment and decision making, regardless of the topic. Exhibit 6.3 shows relative time for decisions, communications, and execution.

Elements of the structure should be changed to meet the needs of a global e-business. New functional areas (e.g., foreign exchange, international tax, international labor law) and resources, whether full-time or part-time employees, consultants, contract workers, and so on, will be needed to compete successfully because the business will change. Companies can retain consultants for tax, global hedging strategies, and cultural and language specialties as specific needs arise. One benefit of enablement is that virtually any function can be outsourced if necessary, and a full-time, permanent employee may not be necessary.

"With the Web, becoming a free agent is no longer limited to athlete, artists, actors, and other big-name professional or creative types. It's now available to almost every kind of knowledge worker. Already the 'free agent' labor pool, including self-employed workers, independent contractors, and workers at temporary agencies, total about 25 million Americans. One benefit of self-employment is diversification—you're less likely to be out of work if you have several employers than if you have one."[42] Organization structure requirements should be analyzed and gaps resolved in a company strategic plan.

Existing Strategy Paradigms

Although a variety of strategic planning processes are available, we will review two well-known planning processes—the business matrix developed by The Boston Consulting Group (BCG) and Michael Porter's theory—because they are thoroughly developed and are used extensively in business. It is not important which strategy process you select but rather how you adapt the strategy to the macro forces of e-business. We will review some of the key elements of the strategy processes to show how enablement and the macro e-business forces can affect strategic planning, your competitor, and the competitive environment.

---

[42] "Business @ the Speed of Thought," by Bill Gates, Warner Books, 1999, New York, p. 137.

Exhibit 6.3

Web-Enabled Structure

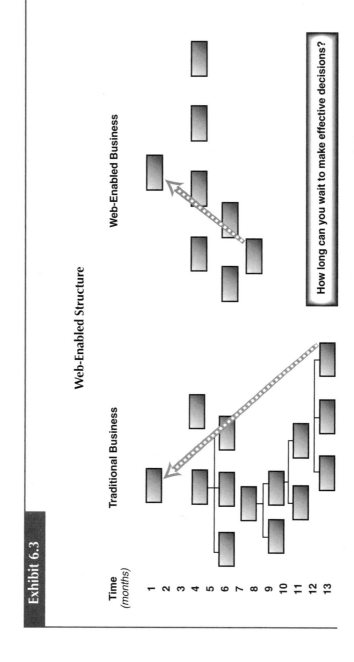

Traditional Business

Web-Enabled Business

Time
(months)

1
2
3
4
5
6
7
8
9
10
11
12
13

How long can you wait to make effective decisions?

120

BCG Strategy Segmentation

BCG developed a strategic framework in the 1970s, which guides management to understand business strengths and weaknesses, the current and expected market characteristics, and the competition. Executives analyze their companies to determine the company's strategic position in a strategy map, which depicts market characteristics, competitor positions, and the results of strategies. Once the framework is complete, executives will develop business plans to increase shareholder value.

The strategic map in Exhibit 6.4 is segmented into four quadrants, each depicting a unique strategic market position with regard to growth and market share.

The *"star"* quadrant represents high-growth, relatively low-market share markets. Companies try to maximize their competitive position in this quadrant for existing or future investments. The Web can change the course of "stars" by accelerating business through new product introductions, can expand sales and market share through new global channels, and can provide instant performance reporting, which allows for better price management, promotional control, and so forth. Hi-tech companies can compound their research capabilities by using the Web to collaborate with others and thereby expand the breadth of potential products; they can also use the Web to accelerate the research and development (R&D) process, moving to higher

Exhibit 6.4

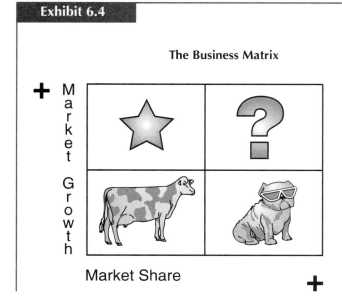

The Business Matrix

Market Growth

Market Share

relevant market share. These actions could not have occurred a decade ago because the Web infrastructure did not exist.

Companies and governments are now investing in the required infrastructure to make the Web more usable. For example, in early 2004, the state of Ohio opened the "Third Frontier Network," which is considered "nothing less than the interstate highway system of the new century . . . The network will allow researchers at one university to view the output of a scientific instrument at a lab hundreds of miles away, which reduces time and costs related to research and development. The MRI Medical Research Magnet at Ohio State University Hospital is the largest in the world. But it generates more than 8 billion bits of data every second—more than 10 times the largest network connection into a university campus in the state . . . With the Third Frontier Network, that amount of information will be easily shared. . . . We can make the entire state a virtual laboratory. . . ."[43]

The *"cash cow"* quadrant represents low market share and low-growth markets. Businesses in this quadrant often fund investments in segments with greater potential value, such as "stars" or "?". The *cash cow* segment is often "milked" by maximizing current cash flow and reducing future investment. Eastman Kodak has defined their photographic film line as a cash cow and will use cash flow from film to fund expected high-value digital imaging. In the "cash cow" segments, enablement can reduce administrative costs in the functions, allowing redeployment of limited resources to higher-value investment opportunities. Improved information flow can also assist in pricing management, inventory control, cash collections, and service.

The *"?"* quadrant represents an unknown market potential in both growth and share potential. Companies often invest carefully in this segment and closely monitor financial results in the early stages to determine whether further investment is warranted. In the late 1990s, the "dot.coms" fell into this segment because results were not proved during the investment period. Unfortunately, the business cycle of dot.coms, from birth to death, ranging from zero market value, to trillions of dollars, to zero, lasted less than a decade. The speed of information in an enabled company will make the assessment of a segment in the "?" area quicker and more effective and will allow for rapid market feedback through the unknown phase. Enablement will improve early-stage sourcing arrangements to minimize initial investments, keep inventories low, and allow for changes in product specifications to improve the market tests.

---

[43] *Cincinnati Enquirer,* Jeannine Aversa, The Associated Press, April 27, 2004, p. 1.

"Dog" markets are low-growth and high-share segments that a company will often divest to redeploy capital to other areas with greater potential. Procter & Gamble divested several of the food and cleaning products businesses in 2003 to redeploy resources to higher-growth segments. Enablement will allow for improved overall management of *dogs* as with all other classifications. But in addition, *dogs* may get renewed life through expanded Web markets/sales, as well as through product analysis. Certain capital-intensive products, although no longer actively marketed, may have service and replacement parts businesses that can be aggressively managed for higher profitability on the Web.

Ideally, a company strategy concentrates investments to maximize the returns—move the "question mark" businesses to a known status, milk the cash cow business to invest in other priorities, and if the business segment is a "dog," divest and redeploy the capital. If you view your business in these quadrants, think about the impact that business pace, open architecture, globalization, education, and organizational structure will have on your company.

Michael Porter—Competitive Strategy

Michael Porter suggests that companies are successful by differentiating using technology or cost leadership because companies trying to do both are not competitive at either strategy. A focused strategy will allow a company to gain the best competitive advantage, better influence or control over the marketplace, and better-than-average returns for the industry. The strategic process is based on the five forces of competition, and the company's position relative to the business cost drivers. The five forces and the potential impact of Web enablement are as follows:

1. *Threat of new entrants:* High barriers to entry will discourage competition. A Web enabled business will change the dynamics of new entrants, as prohibitive cost barriers decline, substitute products proliferate, and the market for customers and vendors is expanded through the Web. An industry or company with an open architecture may actually leapfrog over established businesses because of their complacency and inability to act quickly. For example, digital imaging has changed the entire cost structure of X-ray diagnosis. Not only has digital imaging eliminated the film supply cost, it has also changed the entire cost structure by allowing image analysis to be done by well-trained medical technicians and doctors in low-cost

areas like India. New entrants were created through low-cost global data transmission capabilities.

2. *Industry competitors and rivalry among existing companies:* As companies become Web enabled, the changes in capabilities will destabilize the competitive landscape and change the business strategy. During the past few years, Southwest Airlines has relied heavily on Web-based reservations to improve service and keep costs low. More recently, JetBlue Airways has adopted a program to reduce costs in which employees who telecommute from their homes make all reservations.

3. *Suppliers and bargaining power:* Suppliers and bargaining power will change as a result of the globalization and open architecture of the Web, allowing expanded competition. A workforce in developing countries that works for a fraction of the cost of U.S. employees has changed the competitive landscape in software development, production of electronics equipment, textiles, and toys—virtually any product. Instant engineering and operating information have enabled this disruption and have changed the suppliers' bargaining power as it relates to the entire value chain. JC Penney has shifted authority for product design, manufacture, and supply chain logistics for certain clothing products to a Hong Kong manufacturer. The manufacturer has completely changed the supply value chain.

4. *Buyers and bargaining power:* Buyers and bargaining power will change as a result of the globalization and open architecture of the Web. Global competition, reduced trade barriers, and great disparities in costs around the globe give the buyers a broader array of products, quality, and availability than ever before. During the past decade, instant information has allowed retailers to become more effective by tying point of sale reporting directly to orders at a foreign factory. Elimination of inventory and waste and a smoother business cycle have improved their buying power. Today, the lowest-cost business process and information management have made Wal-Mart the largest global retailer. A major part of their product purchases are now made outside the United States.

5. *Substitute product:* Substitute product or service capability will change because business will now have unlimited access to new technology from all industries and research institutions around the globe.

These five forces must be considered, but the results of the analysis in any industry will now show that their individual relevance is subject to new Web-enablement forces. The Web will be a destabilizing force to change the competitive equilibrium.

Ideally, an effective strategy will create a flow of products/businesses at various stages of their life cycle to have a continuously growing value. Exhibit 6.5 shows how a series of product life cycles at various stages make up a company. Each curve on the chart (A, B, C, etc.) represents an individual product or business. At any point, product sales/profits are increasing, at peak, or declining. The sum of the curves totals a point on the arrow "D," which represents total sales. The ideal business will have many rapidly increasing product curves, with a prolonged "peak" level and a long trail of performance. Using Web forces to create advantage can result in quicker acceleration to peak, more product curves, and prolonged performance with globalization and new ideas. Strategy is the plan that creates more of these curves or prolongs their life cycle.

Business Drivers

Porter has identified *business drivers,* which are often considered the basis of the business cost structure. As we examine these specific business drivers or others that you consider appropriate, we will see how Web enablement has changed their impact on performance, profitability, and value during the past decade. In the new global environment with real-time communications, new aggressive foreign and U.S. competitors will recognize the impact on the business drivers and aggressively change their strategy. The Web can change the perception of being a small or large company to potential customers and suppliers and can also change the performance of a small or large company. Exhibit 6.6 lists the drivers and the potential Web-enablement impact on small and large companies. As you review the drivers, personalize the review and consider how your company—small or large—will be affected by your competitor's Web enablement. I have provided a generic assessment of small or large companies as an example.

Economies of Scale

Economies of scale means getting more results from a specific level of investment. Often, economies of scale are realized in product development or infrastructure activities. Now global access to information and processes changes the impact of economies of scale for all companies. Historically,

Exhibit 6.5

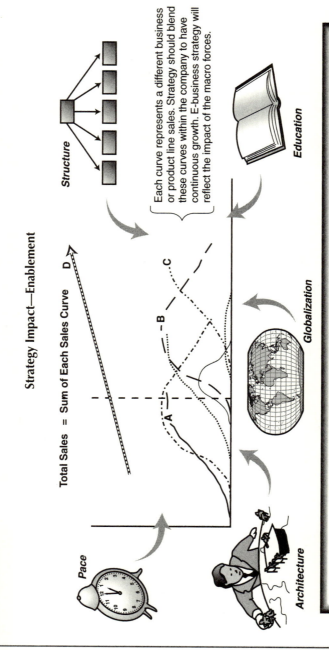

Strategy Impact—Enablement

Total Sales = Sum of Each Sales Curve

Pace

Architecture

Globalization

Education

Structure

Each curve represents a different business or product line sales. Strategy should blend these curves within the company to have continuous growth. E-business strategy will reflect the impact of the macro forces.

Each product has a different life cycle affected by the five macro e-business factors. An effective e-business strategy will embrace each of these factors and accelerate the business processes to improve the business value.

126

Exhibit 6.6

Business Drivers and Web Impact on Competitiveness

Business Drivers	Company Size Large	Small
Economies of scale	⌄	⌃
Learning	⌃	⌃
Pattern of capacity utilization	⌃	⌃
Linkages	⌃	⌃
Interrelationships	⌃	⟩
Integration	⌄	⌄
Timing	⌃	⌃
Policy	⟩	⌃
Location	⌄	⌄
Institutional factors	⟩	⌃

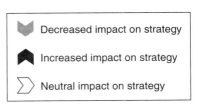

⌄ Decreased impact on strategy

⌃ Increased impact on strategy

⟩ Neutral impact on strategy

Macro Effects of E-Business

	Large	Small
Pace	▮	▮
Architecture	▮	▮
Globalization	▮	▮
Education	▮	▮
Structure	▮	▮

pharmaceutical companies relied heavily on staff scientists for innovation and product development, but now, with instant global access to innovation, scientific know-how is easily within anyone's grasp, from small research companies to U.S. or foreign universities. In the 21st century, historically de-fined economies of scale based on sunk costs in facilities or people will no longer be the critical success factor that it once was; this is because equiva-lent products may be developed and manufactured in low-cost countries for a total landed cost that is a small fraction of that in host countries. If a com-parable part can be produced in China for total cost of 95 percent less than the cost of a mass-produced part in the United States, where is the justification to develop a larger U.S. product development/manufacturing complex that can achieve dramatic economies of scale?

If business processes in competitive companies have shorter cycle times, with equivalent or better quality, and the infrastructure supports the global production and sale of a product, who needs the traditional economies of scale? The economy of scale of owned operations will be minimized in the 21st century because manufacturing and technology can more easily shift to lower cost areas. *Economies of scale will be a process measurement and will measure how well you leverage access to intellectual property, convert information to contracts, engage in joint ventures, and outsource manufacturing.*

Learning

We will define *learning* as a process that increases efficiency as we repeat activities. The first time we build a factory, mistakes will happen; the second time we build a factory, we will make fewer mistakes because of our experience.

Learning is a critical skill in the enabled world, but learning is an experience-based efficiency and a capability. *Experience-based* relates to a concentration of critical skills in any industry and improving a process by repetition. Just as Solectron has become a high-volume electronics production and assembly business for hire, any company can capture its learning by hiring Solectron as a subcontractor, because learning need not be within a company's four walls. The business pace and multiple information sources that we discussed earlier require organizations and personnel (either employees or outsourced) to be capable of rapid and thorough learning. People who are quick learners will be invaluable in the new economy, and in a Web-enabled company, workers can be located anywhere in the world and be full-time, part-time, or contract workers.

Learning will no longer depend on size or repetitive activity when creating a product or service in a company, but rather, *access to learning* will differentiate business.

Pattern of Capacity Utilization

Capacity utilization costs depend on the amount of sunk costs and how effectively we use that investment. Ideally, utilization will be uniform across the business cycle to keep costs low because large changes in throughput usually are very expensive, for example, downsizing or rapidly increasing capacity. If an installed capacity is not used at a proper rate, there will be an economic loss—that is, if only 50 percent of capacity is used, the opportunity cost equals the lost absorption and foregone profits on lost sales. In general, capacity utilization will be better managed in the future using communications, linkages, and intellectual property rights around the globe to smooth utilization. Again, the Web will enable a small or large competitor, anywhere in the world, to be more profitable. Airlines represent an industry that is subject to extraordinary underutilization costs. Large businesses can manage utilization through real-time promotions, scheduling, and load leveling. Smaller businesses can take advantage of their flexibility to acquire capacity to meet their needs without large investments in sunk costs. Airlines have large fixed equipment costs (both owned and leased) and significant investments in personnel, training, and pension costs. The cost per seat-mile varies radically based on their pattern of utilization. Airlines now use historical load factors and real-time "fare-sales" (through Orbitz, Expedia, and Hotwired.com) to better manage their utilization and reduce their economic costs.

Linkages

Linkages are connections between activities in a firm that create additional value. The linkages can develop between both primary and secondary activities to improve value. As product design, manufacturing, and service work together, parts may become more durable and easier to service, allowing companies to give customers more value—and perhaps improved warranties. Linkages can also connect primary and secondary activities to improve value—financial planning and information technology (IT). As financial planning and analysis and the IT department focus on information (sales, manufacturing, warranty, and customer service), data contained in the systems can be mined to provide improved marketing analysis about the customers, products, and so forth, making it possible to improve marketing campaigns. Linkages will expand far beyond the four walls of an e-business company. Linkages will be more important drivers in the new economy because global linkages will reduce barriers to entry for nearly any business, allowing many functions and activities that you now perform to be easily shifted to other organizations. Historically, factors such as travel, qualified personnel, geography, and proximity to raw materials have been obstacles to change. Linkage capabilities will improve performance in both small and large companies.

Interrelationships within a Company

Interrelationships are defined as within a company and generally apply to larger companies. As the business pace rapidly increases outside a company, the *pace of cooperation* within the company must accelerate. Improved interrelationships and knowledge sharing will be critical to companies. For example, during the past decade, Dell has compressed the supply chain by using information within the company to eliminate waste and delay and reduce the supply chain from manufacture to customer to less than 10 days, versus many months in the typical computer supply chain. In a Web-enabled, highly competitive world market, innovation will be accessible to anyone in the world, and large companies must adapt to this change. Inter-relationships can be quickly implemented by using Web tools for communication, collaboration, and research. As companies open their architecture, interrelationships can have a significant impact on performance.

Integration

Historically, the extent of vertical integration often provided exceptional benefits in cost, control, and quality to a large company. Companies controlled the quality, design, and manufacturability of components. Today, however, full integration may be too expensive if the fully integrated company is not the best in the world in the activity or function. In general, unless each function is the best in the world, the greatest cost advantage may go to the smaller, less integrated company. Eventually, activities will migrate to the lowest overall cost of doing business.

Solectron has developed one of the best processes for electronics manufacturing in the world. As a result, companies such as IBM, Dell, Hewlett Packard, and almost any high-volume electronics company buys components from Solectron rather than staff, manage, and provide the capital for an electronics assembly that operates at a less effective rate.

Timing

Timing relates to first mover advantage and late entrants into a product or business. Timing will change a company's strategy because Web enablement creates advantages for both first movers and late entrants. The Web accelerates the pace of business by accelerating both the development cycle and the useable product life cycle times. As product development cycle times accelerate as a result of Web enablement, first mover advantages may be insurmountable in some industries—such as generic pharmaceuticals, where first movers have a legal advantage because the FDA grants short-term exclusivity to new generic formulations of patented drugs. In other industries, first movers must continue the rapid development of products and business to maintain their advantage in a short development cycle Web-enabled world because their advantage equals no more than one cycle.

Late entrants—those immediately following first movers—may also have unique advantages in a Web-enabled world because short cycle times allow competitors to imitate winning products with minimal research effort, source production on short notice, and simply air freight product to the markets (e.g., toys, consumer electronics, fashion clothes). Timing can be an advantage to both small and large companies because communication, research, and transaction processing are accelerated for all who choose to participate. Because timing may be accelerated for both small and large companies, both enjoy the advantages of Web enablement.

Policy

Policy is defined by company management and relates to how it will manage the business. Service levels, business cycle time, human resources choices related to compensation levels and components, product lines, and scope are decisions that will affect your cost structure. Internal policies must be adaptive and allow for flexibility in the workforce—contract or employee—in a Web-enabled business. Because the pace will accelerate and the source of competitive pressure will vary across the globe, it will be impossible for any company to function well without effective policies to guide performance. Policies or broad guidelines, and not rules that can be broken, will be essential in the future and must be well thought-out. Policies may not have been a factor in a small company historically, but the macro effects of the Web may make them essential. Informed and well-trained employees will be critical in the new global environment. A simple policy decision to sell luxury goods may need to be adapted in the new economy to sell luxury goods, in U.S. dollars, to customers who are in locations that do not require changes in warranty, service, or import license and are not subject to value-added tax (VAT) or sales tax.

Location

Historically, location meant proximity to resources or markets. However, with the Web, the economics of global sourcing and selling have changed dramatically. Strategic location will now be *virtual* access to any resource and market, and Web presence will now be the location to create advantage. If we consider proximity to resource (e.g., raw material, trained labor, infrastructure to deliver product or service), location has little relevance to total cost. For example, consider countries such as China, India, and Eastern Europe, which have well-trained employees who earn 90 percent less than comparable U.S. employees. In the service business, knowledge workers such as tax

Exhibit 6.7

Small Company—Examples of Policy Changes

Small Company	Old Paradigm	Web Enabled
Sales		
- Pricing	Sold in U.S. $	Sell in foreign exchange
- Shipping terms	Ship FOB factory	Ship CIF
- Warranties	30 day stated	1 year implied
- Legal	Product liability—U.S.	Product liability—deep pockets
- Import-export	None, except Canada	Canada, Mexico, UK, Spain
Order fulfillment cycle		
- Distribution/distributors	None—all direct	Distributors in foreign countries
- Outsourcing	Easily qualified	Determine how to qualify
* Qualified—financial		
* Qualified—technical		
* Qualified—quality		
Selling, General, & Administrative		
- Product development	U.S. research teams	China universities; universities in Mexico, UK, Spain
* Licensing	U.S. companies	China universities; universities in Mexico, UK, Spain
* Collaboration	U.S. universities	China universities
* Features—country specific	None	Canada, Mexico, UK, Spain
- Advertising	English only	English, Spanish; ethnic for Mexico, Spain, Caribbean
- Regulatory	U.S.	U.S., EU Market
- Overtime	None	Yes—due to time differences
- Telecommuting	None	Yes—due to time differences
- Travel policy	No international	Yes—international required
- Employee training	Limited	Technical, language, and cultural
Assets		
- Make vs. buy	Make or buy option	Buy complete for foreign investment
- Buy vs. lease	Buy	Lease in foreign countries

preparers, programmers, and medical technicians need access to the Web to perform their service. In manufacturing, immediate access to engineering specifications and downloadable machine instructions for production make remote manufacturing a simple risk-free task. IBM has recently hired thousands of knowledge workers in India to develop software. Dell, Accenture, EDS, and other service organizations have also outsourced to India.

Institutional Factors

Institutional factors are rules and regulations outside of the direct influence of a company. Institutional factors such as import/export requirements, agency regulations such as the FDA, Underwriters Laboratories, Federal Trade Commission, or U.S. Department of Defense will now affect more businesses that have access to global markets. Small businesses that historically have never imported/exported may need to be aware of regulations to ensure compliance. Because location may no longer be relevant, institutional factors such as minimum wages, income tax, and Occupational Safety and Health Administration (OSHA) regulations affect the profitability of U.S. business. Small national companies in countries such as China and India may not be affected by such institutional factors, and they may be competing against a U.S. company. How will this affect your strategy? Some companies have chosen to outsource to these foreign sources.

Business drivers will be affected by the new global economy. Companies that recognize the impact on their business strategy will thrive, and those that do not change to reflect enablement will disappear.

Call to Action

We have discussed the impact of the Web on various facets of any planning scenario, but we have not yet clearly stated how to deal strategically with the changes required. The best way to proceed is to develop a matrix of all the functions and business drivers, ranked in importance to your company in its current market position. Rather than try to change all the functions and business drivers at one time, prioritize the possible changes based on impact to your success. Consider the resources required, the benefits and the timing of both the investments and the returns, and the impact on your organization and the constituents. Although the changes may be excellent choices for your businesses, the constituents may not be able to adapt to the changes. If the constituents do not accept the changes, then they will not be permanent. Exhibit 6.8 shows an example of the priorities established in a $100 million electronics manufacturing company.

Exhibit 6.8

Business Drivers—Assessment and Action Plan

Description	Impact	Results Expected	Resp.	Action Required
Scale	▷			
Learning	◀	Rather than invest in new circuit board equipment and training, outsource to third party.	Manufact.	Identify key elements of our board manufacturing. Train buyers re: requirements, foreign exchange, import regulations.
Capacity	▷			
Linkages	◀	Fully integrated board design process with U.S. board producer.		Identify and develop relationships with global third-party electronics company. Coordinate new product development process with third party.
Interrelationships	◀	During new product introductions, create and manage process, which includes customer service, manufacturing, and accounting, to closely manage intro.		Assemble team of leaders from manufacturing, customer service, and accounting to develop charter and process to follow during intro—fast, appropriate information to all critical parties.
Integration	▷			
Timing	▷			
Policy	▷			
Location	▷			
Institutional factors	▷			

Description	Assessment	Function	Activity	Action Plan
Pace	◇			
Architecture	◀	R&D and marketing	Critical functions to expand new product development. Must eliminate NIH (not invented here) attitude.	Hire cultural change expert. Visit other R&D shops to understand how they changed the culture.
Globalization	◇			
Education	◀	R&D	Revise product design activity to include a learning loop that focuses both inside and outside the company.	Outside consultants, new process, and possibly software to improve management of "ideas" and resourced.
Structure	◇			

Summary

In the new economy, all of the basic elements of business will change. The pace, content, and breadth of business will no longer be as in the past, and businesses will lose control over their destiny unless they change how they plan and execute strategies. Although all the strategic elements of a business will remain the same, the environment that affects a business related to each element will change.

The macro e-business forces of pace, architecture, globalization, education, and structure must be reflected in a company strategy, regardless of which paradigm is used to plan. The business cost drivers will affect a business in different ways in the future.

CHAPTER 7

DEVELOPING THE E-BUSINESS PLAN

E-Business Plan—Introduction

In the last few chapters, we have discussed how to analyze your business and develop an e-business strategy that will be successful. We should adapt to the macro e-business factors as soon as possible and integrate them into our business while improving the company's overall value. In this chapter, we will discuss specific plans to implement the strategy by briefly reviewing the e-business process and then reviewing two case studies: a service business and a capital products business. It is important that executives and other influential people within your organization be fully committed to the e-business process. To ensure such commitment, you must make their job easier, provide financial incentives for accomplishing specific objectives while generating more company profits, and create personal accountability, all the while being concerned about the impact of enablement on all of the other constituents.

These are not easy tasks, but considering some of the "quick wins" that we have discussed thus far in travel and entertainment (T&E) costs and usage due to Web meetings, other purchasing, and capacity load management techniques, it is not unreasonable. Savings and business improvements can also be realized in personnel training and administrative areas such as human resources, finance, and legal.

Near-term success generates enthusiasm and also generates profits that can be reinvested in the enablement process. Be careful that you do not use enablement simply to cut costs because cost cutting represents a small portion of the benefit. Enablement is an attitude as well as a technology that will permeate the entire organization.

Once you have prioritized the early wins, concentrate on several of the macro e-business factors—pace, architecture, globalization, education, and structure—for sustained business improvement. Select programs that enable your business on a prioritized basis because trying to implement too many programs simultaneously will dilute your efforts.

Last, as you develop the implementation plans and begin execution, make the goals public after you gain consensus with the executive team.

Measure performance and publicly report your progress to keep the organization focused.

The Process

As a brief refresher, we will do the planning by following the previously discussed process:

- *Team:* Assemble a team of the best people because this process could very well determine the success of your company. The team should include a lead executive who has been trained in the art of enablement and the best personnel from the affected departments or constituent groups. If outside organizations are involved, understand that it may be difficult to enroll them in the process unless you create an advantage for them—such as reduced costs, higher selling prices, faster payment cycles, and so forth.

- *Analysis and assessment:* Prepare baseline summaries that contain the critical elements to measure as programs are implemented. The summaries should include profit and loss (P&L) information, balance sheet information, and perhaps cash flow summaries; in some cases, you may also want to include nonfinancial data, such as business cycle time, and units of measure, such as number of work orders, customers, vendors, and so forth. At times, although you would like to have exact data, informed estimates may serve you better because they can be more easily obtained. If you have access to reasonable estimates, use the information to begin the analysis rather than postponing the entire implementation for complete details.

- *Plan:* The plan is the best estimate of how and when you will perform a task and the amount and timing of the costs and benefits of the tasks. This is not a cost-cutting exercise, but a value improvement process, which may involve some cost cutting—ideally for redeployment to value-added activities. The plan should have sufficient detail to measure results, determine success or failure, and determine the root cause of variance from the plan. Examples will be discussed later in the chapter in the two case studies.

- *Execution:* Assigned personnel (inside or outside the company) will have specific tasks to complete, within the stated time frame and costs. Monitoring systems should be developed to ensure that reasonable controls are in effect.

We will review two case studies that reflect the principles discussed. Throughout the analysis and planning, we will focus on economic value, which can be a reduced cost to the company; the value of a resource that can be redeployed to a higher value-added activity; or increased sales/profits. I have defined economic value this way to further reinforce the fact that Web enablement does not have a primary goal of cost cutting.

Baseline Business Summary

Key strategic deliverables will be those few items that you implement within the planning horizon that are the basis of long-term Web-enablement success. Because an enabled business moves more quickly than most traditional businesses, the initial deliverables will be achieved early in a typical strategic plan, that is, in the first 12 months. The previous analysis of functions, activities, and costs and opportunities will be the guide to establishing strategic priorities. Actual planned tactics will support these strategic goals.

The strategies selected will depend on your business and its relative competitive position. We will examine case studies for a global service company and for a global industrial products manufacturer to demonstrate the analysis and prioritization of plans to make an organization Web enabled.

First, prepare a brief financial summary of the business that includes the functional and activity summaries discussed in earlier chapters. This is not a review to highlight poor performance, but one that will highlight major opportunities. The financial summary will include benchmark information from competitive businesses and businesses that are the best in the world in particular functions. If you benchmark only against your competitors, you will miss those breakthroughs that will redefine your industry or company. The case study financial summaries in Exhibit 7.1 will examine a service and a capital business separately and should be reviewed with the key executives who are responsible for enablement before plans are finalized. You will identify enablement opportunities by asking, "What is done today?"; approaching the business from the *enablement* perspective makes it possible to identify new opportunities. What better way to feel empowered than by developing some of the first benefits as you initially prepare the analysis?

Exhibit 7.1 includes financial data, ratios, and other relevant information (e.g., head count, work orders processed, number of customers). The lead executive should identify relevant performance measures to understand the business, knowing that the measures may change based on the company's competitive position. For example, in the first year, warranty costs may be monitored, whereas in the second year, service contract renewals may be most

Exhibit 7.1

Case Study—Financial Summary

| | Service | | Capital | | Benchmark Ratios | |
	Amount (Millions $)	% of Sales	Amount (Millions $)	% of Sales	Service % of Sales	Capital % of Sales
Sales	200.0	100.0%	800	100.0%	55.0%	50.0%
Gross Profit	80.0	40.0%	360	45.0%		
SG&A						
Sales	20.0	10.0%	80	10.0%	7.0%	7.0%
Marketing	10.0	5.0%	30	3.8%	5.0%	3.0%
R&D	15.0	7.5%	65	8.1%	7.5%	10.0%
Finance	7.0	3.5%	21	2.6%	3.0%	2.5%
Other Administrative	8.0	4.0%	30	3.8%	2.0%	2.0%
Total SG&A	60.0	30.0%	226.0	28.3%	24.5%	24.5%
Profit Before Tax	20.0	10.0%	134.0	16.8%	30.5%	25.5%
Fixed Assets	30.0		100.0			
Inventory	50.0		200.0			
Accounts Receivable	40.0		200.0			
Head Count						
Direct	700		2,500			
Indirect	210		1,500			
Total	910		4,000			
Asset Intensity	25%		25%		20%	15%
Inventory Turns	2.4		2.2		15	18
Days Sales Outstanding	90		90		50	30
# of Service Orders	540,000		n/a			
# of Service Contracts	1,590		n/a			
# of Active Customers	5,250		1,250			
Sales per Head Count	219,780		200,000			
# BOMs			1500			
# of Shop Workorders			17500			

important. Once the key variables have been identified, obtain benchmark data from competitors and industry statistics; if no other data are available, use historical trends to benchmark against. Exhibit 7.1 also includes balance sheet information because enablement will accelerate the billing process and reduce receivables. Creating additional free cash flow is an excellent benefit of enablement; although the direct measurable P&L impact may be limited to a relatively small interest expense reduction, firm value will improve. The exhibit also includes the vertical ratios and expenses (expressed as a percentage of sales), which are relative performance measures in any business. Once the template of required information is defined, if all the information that you require is not available, rather than delaying the entire project, use estimates and summarize actual information at a scheduled later date.

An excellent example of how to apply measurement to the new e-business company is eBay. "Another saying around eBay's headquarters is, if it moves, measure it. Whitman personally monitors a host of barometers. There are the standard ones for Internet companies: how many people are visiting the site, how many of those then register to become users, how long each user remains per visit, how long pages take to load, and on and on. Whitman also closely eyes eBay's 'take rate', the ratio of revenues to the value of goods traded on the site (the higher the better). She measures which days are busiest, the better to determine when to offer free listings in order to stimulate the supply of auction items. (Mondays in June are slow; Fridays in November rock.) She even monitors the 'noise' on eBay's discussion boards, online forums where users discuss, among other things, their opinion of eBay's management. (Level 1 means 'silent', and 10 means 'hot' or, in Webb's words, 'the community is ready to kill you.' Normal for eBay is about 3.) In other words, eBay is a fire hose of business data."[44]

Service Business Description—Case Study

In the service business, fax machines and telephones are used to schedule customer service. Cell phones or pagers are used to request urgent service from the technicians, but technicians are not required to reply within a specified time. There are about 100 service centers around the country, staffed by five to seven service representatives each.

Service work orders are handwritten, and the technician records parts and labor used based on his or her best recollection at the end of the workday. Parts are occasionally omitted from the completed work order, as evidenced

[44] "Meg and the Machine," by Adam Lashinsky, *Fortune,* September 1, 2003, pp. 68–78.

by the inventory shortages at the periodic physical inventories and the number of "rush" overnight shipments required by out-of-stock parts. Work orders are often completed back at the office after normal work hours or early the next morning, resulting in longer workdays for technicians. The customer provides little feedback about the quality of the service, timeliness, or presentability of the technician.

Warranty work is captured on the work orders if coded properly, but there is no central control point to capture and analyze the product warranty cost. Occasionally, someone at the headquarters office will focus on the service department's low profitability compared with a well-run service organization and will then prepare a one-of-a-kind profit analysis.

Work order time summaries for service technicians are prepared at the end of the week and faxed to the headquarters office for data entry by the payroll department. No performance analysis is completed because the data entered are limited to the time spent on "chargeable" time to clients. Warranty and contract work is not managed because there is no time to do so. If the service representative forgets or chooses not to record the charges, or forgets to record a special favor for a favorite client, there is little check-or-balance to monitor this free service. As a result of the lack of information, the company has been reluctant to sell service contracts to customers because profitability is unknown. The service function is considered a necessary evil to sell the equipment and keep the customers happy and is perceived as a cost center, not a profit center.

The Process

As we review this service business, many opportunities for improvement exist, including revenue increases, cost decreases, and possible resource redeployment. Because the 40 percent gross margin for a service organization is below benchmark data, we should analyze how the service technicians are spending their time—fee-for-service, service contract, warranty, and other—because technicians are expensive to maintain when you consider wages, benefits, and travel as cost and time as an opportunity cost.

Exhibit 7.2 summarizes the first level of review in the service organization. To develop an *enablement plan,* we must look at the functional spending and the actual activities performed, knowing that we can improve the business using the Web. Although actual *direct* spending (incurred in performance of service to the customer) is heavily weighted at the department spending level, we should closely examine the actual activities performed within *direct* spending to be sure that the classification is correct. Then we

Exhibit 7.2

Functional Analysis—Service Department

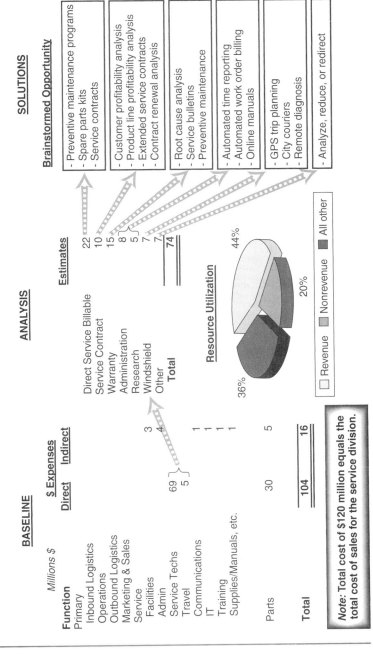

BASELINE

$ Expenses

Millions $

Function	Direct	Indirect
Primary		
Inbound Logistics		
Operations		
Outbound Logistics		
Marketing & Sales		
Service	69 }	5
Facilities		3
Admin		4
Service Techs		
Travel		1
Communications		1
IT		1
Training		1
Supplies/Manuals, etc.		
Parts	30	5
Total	**104**	**16**

Note: Total cost of $120 million equals the total cost of sales for the service division.

ANALYSIS

Estimates

Direct Service Billable	22
Service Contract	10
Warranty	15
Administration	8 }
Research	5
Windshield	7
Other	7
Total	**74**

Resource Utilization

44%

36%

20%

☐ Revenue ☐ Nonrevenue ■ All other

SOLUTIONS

Brainstormed Opportunity

- Preventive maintenance programs
- Spare parts kits
- Service contracts

- Customer profitability analysis
- Product line profitability analysis
- Extended service contracts
- Contract renewal analysis

- Root cause analysis
- Service bulletins
- Preventive maintenance

- Automated time reporting
- Automated work order billing
- Online manuals

- GPS trip planning
- City couriers
- Remote diagnosis

- Analyze, reduce, or redirect

should benchmark to competitors, other service industries, and company history to improve customer service and competitiveness.

Exhibit 7.2 further segments direct service and travel costs into specific activities performed by the technicians. The summary should be prepared using qualified estimates; if estimates are not available, use detailed time and accounting studies. The brainstorming portion of the analysis represents considerable potential change for the service department because new skills may be required and their traditional work content and patterns may change.

Review and Brainstorming

Examine all the functional areas involved in any effective service operation and be sure to look outside your organization; failure to do so may result in missed opportunities. For example, service billings may be prepared and sent automatically without any review or special handling in your company. At another service company, however, service contract files may be cross-referenced to the customer billing and the invoice will include a note reminding the customer that the service contract renewal is upcoming. An e-mail may also be automatically sent to the territory sales representative for follow-up. If you do not look outside the four walls, you will never be aware of such possible improvements. Discuss problems and opportunities with other high-quality service organizations to see what can be done to improve service ability, uptime performance, and customer service.

In the case study, a major part of the service department cost, driven by the technician's time, is spent behind the windshield, responding to warranty claims and delivering service on a fee basis. Another major block of the technician's time is used to complete paperwork (administration), research service manuals, and perform other unclassified activities. None of the technician's time is devoted to "selling" service contracts to the customers. Because it is likely that the technicians have established relationships with the customers and may be trusted by the customers, selling service contracts may be a missed opportunity. Technicians are also on site to examine the installed equipment and can provide the sales representative with a status report of the equipment and competitor's products. A brief e-mail, perhaps with a digital picture attached, may alert the sales organization to a major sales opportunity. Of course, any digital images of customer locations should be cleared with the client before transmitting throughout your organization.

In this example, less than 60 percent of the technician's time is actually spent fixing the equipment; 40 percent of the time is spent on other activities. If we can add 10 percent to technicians' productive time, we have effectively added 70 technicians (700 technicians at 10 percent improvement) to the company without spending a single additional dollar. Our challenge is to convert the highly trained technician's time from administrative and other efforts to value-added service or selling time, or in this case to reduce warranty, administration, and other time using the Web. Possible value improvements are listed in Exhibit 7.2. Some quick hits that may improve value follow:

- Wireless PDAs to order parts and invoice work orders
- Online shop manuals for remote problem diagnosis
- Urgent service bulletins to alert customers to product failures
- Online training to assist customers with equipment problems and self-diagnosis
- Online, real-time inventory for order/delivery scheduling

The technician often does not have the proper parts on hand, which may require multiple visits. Improved inventory control through wireless real-time ordering should reduce this non-value-added time. Also, monitoring repair trends, kitting parts for commonly used product failures, and hiring a local delivery service to have the parts on hand when required will reduce this non-value-added time. As we analyze the parts inventories at all locations, we may find that some service centers are never out of parts—however, the service centers may stock several hundred thousand dollars' worth of parts. Too much inventory in the wrong place does not serve all customers well. Online perpetual inventories accessible to the technicians on a wireless system will improve service throughout the country and reduce overall inventory. Even if only the top 100 items were managed online, the company would achieve a significant financial advantage. There is no need to do *all or nothing* with any of these proposed activities because part of a solution may give you the majority of benefit every time.

Customers, including offshore distributors, may become more involved in the service process when we have a completely enabled service organization, that is, performing self-diagnostic service procedures using guidelines available on the Web or responding to surveys. If we expect customers to become enabled, communications must be simple and we may need to provide incentives to them and train them.

In all cases, the customers and the offshore representatives should be trained to access and read the service bulletins that will be offered periodically. To be effective, we may need an incentive to encourage them to access our website. For example, registering basic information on the site will make them eligible for a small gift such as a free PDA.

As we examine the changes in activity, enablement is initially extra work for the technicians. You may have to compensate or provide incentives to the technicians for their additional efforts. Examples could include cash bonuses when certain training levels have been achieved or possibly commissions when service agreements have been signed. Quite often, a website posting territory growth rates, profitability ratios, or service time will encourage a more competitive environment.

Once the brainstorming is completed, estimate the costs and benefits of the programs to understand the company impact; then select the plans that meet your short- and long-term goals. In Exhibit 7.3, five programs are listed—two cost reduction, one customer improvement, and two value-added programs. Projects are also identified as Tact (tactical) or Macro (e-business macro impact) as another way to view the business improvement projects.

The summary includes quarterly timelines for implementation and expected financial results. You may also want to include a column for probability to help prioritize the programs—a million dollar benefit with a low probability is less valuable than a $500,000 benefit with a high probability. These summaries will help you balance the company impact of the various programs by understanding the P&L and cash flow impact of the programs; if necessary, make sure that the enablement is self-funding. The summary also includes a column that shows responsibility to ensure complete accountability. These departments should be part of the development cost, benefit, and time estimation process. Some notes on the side also indicate how insignificant these changes actually are while the company realizes a major benefit. In the case study, these simple changes add more than $2 million to earnings annually, and we did not terminate a single employee to get the savings.

Macro Analysis—Service Business

Once some of the detailed plans have been prepared to identify the financial benefits of enablement, we can better assess how much cash/expense is available to invest to address the macro impact of the Web. There is no preferred prioritization method of detail versus macro analysis because both must be done. However, it is easier to accept change if people can see and measure a tangible benefit. The macro analysis really addresses the company's strategic environment affected by pace, architecture, globalization, education, and structure. The team and brainstorming techniques used on the individual projects should be used to address the macro Web enablement impacts as well.

Exhibit 7.3

Program Planning

(Millions $)

Ref	Description	Responsible	Year 1 Q1	Year 1 Q2	Year 1 Q3	Year 1 Q4	Year 2 Q1	Year 2 Q2	Year 2 Q3	Year 2 Q4
1—Tact	**Supply purchases concentrated with one vendor**	Purchasing	(0.05)							
	Benefit			0.05	0.05	0.05	0.05	0.05	0.05	0.05
	Project subtotal		*(0.05)*	*0.05*	*0.05*	*0.05*	*0.05*	*0.05*	*0.05*	*0.05*
2—Tact	**Install VOIP to eliminate long-distance charges**	IT								
	Benefit			(0.20)	0.07	0.07	0.07	0.07	0.07	0.07
	Project subtotal		*(0.05)*	*(0.13)*	*0.07*	*0.07*	*0.07*	*0.07*	*0.07*	*0.07*
3—Tact	**Analyze warranty; Pareto losses; implement reporting**	Finance								
	Benefit				(0.20)	0.10	0.40	0.40	0.40	0.50
	Project subtotal				*(0.10)*	*0.40*	*0.40*	*0.40*	*0.40*	*0.50*
4—Macro	**Implement real-time work order reporting**	Service								
	Benefit					(0.10)	(0.40)	0.20	0.20	0.20
	Project subtotal					*(0.10)*	*(0.20)*	*0.20*	*0.20*	*0.20*
5—Macro	**Implement real-time billing**	Finance								
	Benefit						(0.20)	0.10	0.10	0.10
	Project subtotal						*(0.20)*	*0.10*	*0.10*	*0.10*
	Quarterly Total		**(0.05)**	**(0.08)**	**0.12**	**0.52**	**0.22**	**0.82**	**0.82**	**0.92**
	Cumulative (Investment) Saving		**(0.05)**	**(0.13)**	**(0.01)**	**0.51**	**0.73**	**1.55**	**2.37**	**3.29**

Cost -- ▧ Customer ++ ▨ Employee ++

Future Programs
- Digital photos for remote service diagnosis
- Video conferencing and digital camcorders to observe working equipment to assist in remote diagnosis
- Data streaming to track real-time equipment performance
- Expanded international distribution system due to global training capabilities; online service manuals
- Wireless GPS

(continued)

147

Exhibit 7.3 *Continued*

Program Planning

Ref	Year 3 Quarter 1	2	3	4	Cumulative	Average Saving/Year	Probability	Quick Notes
1—Tact	0.05	0.05	0.05	0.05	(0.05) 0.55			Studies indicate up to 27% of supply costs will be saved.
	0.05	*0.05*	*0.05*		*0.50*	0.17	H	
2—Tact	0.07	0.07	0.07	0.07	(0.20) 0.77			In fact, long-distance costs go to ZERO, and 100% to be saved.
	0.07	*0.07*	*0.07*		*0.57*	0.21	H	
3—Tact	0.50	0.50	0.60	0.60	(0.20) 4.40			Represents less than 3% of warranty costs.
	0.50	*0.50*	*0.60*		*4.20*	1.68	M	
4—Macro	0.20	0.20	0.20	0.20	(0.50) 1.90			Represents 2% of administrative costs charged.
	0.20	*0.20*	*0.20*		*1.40*	0.56	H	
5—Macro	0.10	0.10	0.10	0.10	(0.40) 0.90			Represents the estimated value of lost charges due to billing delays.
	0.10	*0.10*	*0.10*		*0.50*	0.22	L	
	0.92	**0.92**	**1.02**	**1.02**	**7.17**	**2.39**		
	4.21	**5.13**	**6.15**	**7.17**				

Cost --   Customer ++   Employee ++

Pace

We should never be satisfied with the pace of our business, and we should always strive to improve customer service and competitiveness and minimize downtime or non-revenue-producing activity. Accelerating the business pace will encourage the service technicians to eliminate non-value-added work and improve the overall profitability.

Non-value-added activity in this example includes manual preparation of time sheets by the technicians, faxing information to the headquarters office for compilation (both work orders and time sheets), and service manual research to determine how to service the equipment.

Also, the service business is not properly analyzed because so few data are captured. If we analyze further, we will see that revenue-producing activity accounts for only 44 percent of the technician's time and non-revenue-producing activity (warranty) and all other activities represent 56 percent of the time. Ideally, we should accelerate the reporting processes through the Web, initially using outsourced software applications through an ASP for time and work order preparation, parts usage, and so forth. Using the Web with wireless communications allows accurate reporting to load the time, work order, and inventory databases for billing, payroll, and analysis. In this example, automating these processes will significantly reduce the $8 million of administrative cost, allowing for revenue improvement and/or cost reductions, and will also reduce the possibility of unbilled parts and service. Having sufficient detail in work descriptions will also give reliable information to analyze warranty, service costs, inventory replenishment, and so forth, thereby allowing for additional improvements.

Architecture

Open the service department's architecture to encourage and accept the feedback available from all constituents. Quickly communicating service problems (e.g., excessive warranty costs, parts shortages) to both the service and manufacturing function will improve overall customer service by providing advance service bulletins, product improvements through both design and manufacturing, and improved logistics. Once effective open communication is established, analyses can be prepared to improve the company's competitive performance in each area.

Feedback from the customers on specific work orders will improve the service department's function. Simple Web feedback mechanisms such as message boards or perhaps automatically generated follow-up surveys will provide quick access to customer feedback. A Web-enabled open architecture will also encourage the offshore distributors to report product observations (e.g., manufacturing quality, design) to headquarters for analysis and improvement. The communication can range from a simple bulletin board, to a more sophisticated survey that includes specific questions and performance criteria, digital photos, and real-time performance data. Direct communication on the Web can be *fast, unedited, unbiased, and available for management review immediately, as well as easily summarized to analyze trends by product, technician, territory, and so forth.*

Global

Except for the communication that may be helpful for the existing offshore distributors, there is no immediate plan for expanding the service operation globally. Timely service bulletins will assist the offshore distributors to improve their customer service. As Web education, training, and service manuals are developed, it is more practical and profitable to expand globally because the service infrastructure will be available to support expanded territories. Once a service website is established, the company should be prepared to respond to questions from any location where the equipment is installed, whether it be China, India, Russia, Brazil, or any other country.

Education

Education can range from cultural to technical to service support training. Service technicians and management should be trained to provide and accept constructive comments about the products and services in response to the open architecture. As specific Web applications are developed, technicians and management should also be trained to use the applications effectively—for example, how to report work orders, time reporting, and supply requests using a wireless PDA. In each case, this training can be completed using a combination of personal training and *Web-cast training.* Online coursework and automatic employee personnel file maintenance and monitoring can also be available for specific technical improvements that arise. Product education discussing some of the unique features of the products can also be available for customers—no matter where in the world— through Web casts. Service manuals can also be maintained online to educate customers, distributors, and potential customers, improve equipment service time, and actually create a competitive advantage.

Structure

As we implement improvements driven by Web applications, the organization's structure and job responsibilities will change because many of the non-value-added tasks will be eliminated, although people may not necessarily be terminated. Intermediaries whose job has been to report/input data may no longer be required or a smaller staff may be required. For example, clerks that input the work order data and the time sheet information may be retrained to analyze trends and prepare summaries of specific information or to analyze specific service, warranty, and customer trends—information based on customer size, locations, and so forth. These same clerks may also schedule service contract renewals, analyze data for specific profitability trends, telemarket to existing and potential customers, and so on. The organization should redeploy the time recovered from non-value-added tasks or eliminate the unnecessary resources.

Manufacturing and Capital Business—Case Study

The company has $800 million of sales, distributed among the United States, Europe, and distributors. Machines are priced from about $500 to nearly $50,000. Low-end machines are often viewed as virtually disposable (they are never repaired because the cost of repair is too high), whereas the high-end machines require nearly 100 percent productive time and timely repair is essential. Today, the company awaits infrequent calls from service to respond to technical problems. The organization has sales support teams that travel the countryside to identify sales opportunities. A sales force of nearly 400 representatives, staff support, and management cover the United States. Other personnel are listed in Exhibit 7.4.

The company has identified several troubling cost areas that seem to have increased over the past few years:

- Warranty costs have been climbing by about 25 percent per year for the past 3 years.
- The number of inventory turns has been declining while service levels to the customers continue to decline.
- Days' sales outstanding (DSO) have been flat at about 90 DSOs during the past 3 years.
- New products have been slow to develop and introduce and are not well received by the customer as in the past.

Although the company has not confirmed the analysis, it seems that more of the offshore business is coming from Europe, while our main competitors

Exhibit 7.4

Functional Analysis—Manufacturing Operations

BASELINE

Millions $

Function	Direct	Indirect
Primary		
Inbound Logistics		
Operations		
Direct Labor	130	40 ⌉
Admin/Indirect		39
Facilities		15
Travel		3
Communications		6
IT		6
Training		4
Supplies/Manuals, etc.		22
Other		15
Outbound Logistics		
Marketing & Sales		
Service		
Materials/Assemblies	160	
Total	**290**	**150**

ANALYSIS

Estimates

Assembly	125
Health Insurance	22
Shift Premium	12
Overtime	14
Repair/Rework	18
Supervision	18
Total	**209**
Raw Mat'l—U.S.	38
Raw Mat'l—Other	3
Components—U.S.	57
Components—Other	12
Subassemblies—U.S.	32
Subassemblies—Other	8
Shrinkage	10
Total	**160**

SOLUTIONS

Brainstormed Opportunity

- Smoothe workflow to reduce second shift and overtime.

- Consider health care admin. costs to reduce overall cost.
- Consider health care online bidding to reduce costs/maintain benefits.

- Root cause analysis on repair/rework to reduce cost.

- Consider online bidding for commodity products and raw mat'l.

- Collaborative design for improved products and minimal rework.

Total cost of $440 million equals the total cost of sales for the manufacturing division.

152

Research & Development

Personnel	25	
Consulting	7	
IT	7	
Supplies, etc.	3	
Travel	3	
Prototypes	10	
Other	4	
Total	**52**	

6
3
4
13

Design—Direct
Design—Project Management
Dept. Administration
Communications/Meetings
Prototypes—Inhouse
Prototypes—Outsourced

22
6
2
1
8
2

- Collaborative design for improved products and reduced cycle time.

- Web-enabled project management ASP for global project management.

- Outsourced specialty prototypes to improve cycle time, state-of-the-art resources.

have enjoyed significant growth in the Far East and modest growth in Europe. Competitors have also established distribution in Latin America, a region that the company has been unable to penetrate thus far.

The Process

As we review this manufacturing business, many opportunities for improvement exist, including potential revenue increases, cost decreases, and possible resource redeployment. The 45 percent gross margin for manufacturing is below benchmark data, with particularly high costs in repair/rework and inventory shrinkage. Premium accessories and offshore margins are below the historical trends and seem to be below competitive ratios.

Exhibit 7.4 summarizes the first level of review in the manufacturing organization. We will develop an enablement plan by reviewing the current business and considering all the potential benefits of the Web. Although actual *direct* spending (i.e., costs incurred manufacturing product for the customer) is heavily weighted at the department spending level (Exhibit 7.4), we will closely examine the actual activities performed within *direct* to be sure that the classification is correct. Then we will benchmark to competitors, other manufacturing industries, and actual history to better understand the company performance.

As we examine the costs incurred, we see that we spend $44 million for shift premium, overtime, and repair/rework. Although these may be direct costs, they represent spending premiums for shift and overtime work that may be reduced or eliminated if we smooth the production process. Repair and rework are also non-value-added costs that can be eliminated if we correct the process failures that generate these costs. Further examination of the summary shows that most materials, components, and subassemblies are sourced almost exclusively in the United States, which may result in higher costs than can be obtained offshore or through consolidation of vendors. Product sales analysis will show that few new customers have been acquired in the Far East and Europe and no new customers have been acquired in Latin America.

The Review and Brainstorming

Costs   Compare the metrics of the functional areas in the manufacturing company to those in similar and vastly different manufacturing industries because you may miss opportunities unless you look beyond your current industry. These credible external sources of new ideas and successful enablement will help convince personnel in your company that change can actually be implemented.

In this case study, pretax earnings total $134 million and immediate profit opportunities such as shift premium, overtime, and repair total $44 million, or more than 30 percent of realized profit. In the manufacturing area, "lean business" principles often create major benefits when using the Web. If a company can smooth the production cycle using customer promotional incentives and modified bonus and commission plans to influence order timing and delivery dates, real economic gains will be realized. Through real-time production load balancing and dynamic scheduling (i.e., reacting to the current order activities), production peaks can be smoothed and the shift premium and overtime pay can be reduced.

Repair and rework represent a process failure. First identify the root cause of the failure, which may be researched on the factory floor (for those items that failed during the production process) or through customer service (for those items that failed in the field). Field service technicians may be the first source of analytical data, which could include digital photos, machine diagnostic information transmitted wirelessly to the factory engineers, or on-site observations by the technician. Quick, thorough communication will prevent additional failures by changing the process, materials, or design and will save future warranty and repair cost while improving customer satisfaction.

Materials, component, and subassembly sourcing are often areas to save money through consolidation of vendors or outsourcing processes to third parties. These costs total $150 million and include a mix of high- and low-tech items. Although outsourcing may have many negative connotations for U.S. employees, if the identical or better-quality components/materials with comparable design can be delivered on an acceptable schedule by using a supplier 5,000 miles distant but at a cost of 30 to 40 percent less, management must consider the alternative. The Web communication environment, design collaboration with businesses that specialize in product areas, and off-shore expertise that may equal or exceed the U.S. resources require that we investigate offshore sources more thoroughly. As we examine the potential for online design capabilities and computer-controlled production, design and production cycle time may actually be better than that experienced within the company.

Managing global projects is complex and time-consuming. Web project management tools, Web conferencing software, and access to technical expertise anywhere in the world makes effective coordination possible, whereas before the Web, such project management was impossible. Time, travel costs, and employee inconvenience will be minimal using Web tools.

Revenue We have the opportunity to better manage revenues through sales promotions, incentives, and sales programs that sell individual products or "bundles" of higher-margin accessories and service contracts or perhaps even clear inventory of obsolete products. In each case, real-time information about order cancellations, inventory levels, product returns, or available manufacturing capacity will enhance both revenue and profits. Although such programs were possible before the Web, the Web makes these high-value programs accessible to almost any business.

Web-enabled research and development (R&D) design and automated production capabilities will reduce design-to-market cycle time, which improves value through early product introduction and premium pricing. In the case study, the design is done in-house. Often, the offshore engineer's qualifications equal those of the U.S. engineer, but costs are much less, allowing us to outsource at no incremental cost. Access to global engineering resources will allow a company to easily access experts that may be outside the core technology of current employees. For example, in the liquid crystal display (LCD) industry, several different technologies are involved in designing the product—some of which may not be available as employees on the company staff. The Web enables the successful collaboration with many other industries and universities to solve technical problems.

Using the Web, the company can also expand Latin American sales through Web promotion directed to the end-user or through distributors identified in trade organizations researched on the Web.

Assets As we examine the manufacturing company, we also see that the Web can improve inventory and accounts receivable levels through better real-time management. For example, if the manufacturing operation can deliver product in a shorter order-to-fulfillment cycle to the customer, the company may be able to reduce the billing terms from Net 30 to Net 15, reduce the accounts receivable balance, and improve cash flow. With real-time information, inventory management processes, sales promotions, and just-in-time (JIT) manufacturing processes will be implemented more successfully.

Exhibit 7.5 presents an example of a plan. Once the plan brainstorming is complete, estimate the costs and benefits of the programs to understand the total company impact and select the plans that meet your short- and long-term goals. In Exhibit 7.5, six programs are listed—two cost reduction, two asset improvement, one sales program, and one product development program. The summary includes quarterly timelines for implementation and

Exhibit 7.5

Manufacturing Program Planning

(Millions $)

Ref	Description	Responsible	Year 1				Year 2			
			1	2	3	4	1	2	3	4
1—Tact	**Concentrate mat'ls purchases: fewer vendors**	Purchasing								
	Benefit		(0.10)	(0.10)	(0.10)	0.50	0.50	0.60	0.60	0.60
	Project subtotal		(0.10)	–	0.40	0.50	0.50	0.60	0.60	0.60
2—Tact	**Business cycle management; OT; shift prem.**	Operations								
	Benefit		(0.10)	–	0.10	0.10	0.10	0.20	0.20	0.30
	Project subtotal		(0.10)	–	0.10	0.10	0.10	0.20	0.20	0.30
3—Macro	**Accelerate new product development**	R&D								
	Benefit		(0.10)	(0.10)	(0.10)	0.40	0.50	0.50	0.50	0.80
	Project subtotal		(0.10)	–	0.10	0.40	0.50	0.50	0.50	0.80
4—Macro	**Inventory levels—obsolescence improvement**	Logistics								
	Benefit		(0.10)	0.10	0.10	0.10	0.20	0.20	0.20	0.20
	Project subtotal		(0.10)	–	0.10	0.10	0.20	0.20	0.20	0.20
5—Macro	**Accounts receivable DSO improvement**	Finance								
	Benefit		–	–	–	(0.30)	–	–	–	–
	Project subtotal		–	–	–	(0.30)	–	–	–	–
6—Tact	**Sales to Latin America**	Sales								
	Benefit		(0.10)	(0.10)	(0.10)	0.05	0.20	0.30	0.30	0.30
	Project subtotal		(0.10)	–	(0.05)	0.20	0.30	0.30	0.30	0.30
	Quarterly Total		(0.10)	(0.30)	0.20	1.00	1.30	1.50	1.50	1.90
	Cumulative (Investment) Saving		(0.40)	(0.20)		0.80	2.10	3.60	5.10	7.00

Cost -- | R&D Product Dev. | Asset Reduction | Sales

(continued)

Exhibit 7.5 Continued

Manufacturing Program Planning

Ref	Year 3				Cumulative	Average Saving/Year	Quick Notes
	1	2	3	4			
1—Tact	0.70	0.70	0.70	0.80	(0.30)		
					6.30		
	0.70	0.70	0.70	0.80	6.00	2.00	Represents less than 2% of spending.
2—Tact	0.30	0.30	0.30	0.30	(0.10)		
					2.20		
	0.30	0.30	0.30	0.30	2.10	0.76	Represents about 5% of OT and shift premium.
3—Macro	0.80	0.80	0.90	0.90	(0.20)		
					6.20		
	0.80	0.80	0.90	0.90	6.00	2.40	Represents new product value of less than 2% of base.
4—Macro	0.20	0.20	0.20	0.20	(0.10)		
					1.90		
	0.20	0.20	0.20	0.20	1.80	0.72	Represents reduced obsolescence due to Web sales programs.
5—Macro	–	–	–	–	(0.30)		
					–		
	–	–	–	–	(0.30)	(0.13)	$10 million annual cash flow increase of 5% due to accounts receivable reduction.
6—Tact	0.50	0.50	0.50	0.80	(0.30)		
					3.75		
	0.50	0.50	0.50	0.80	3.45	1.38	Expand sales to annual rate of $2+ million.
	2.00	2.00	2.10	2.20	15.30		
	9.00	11.00	13.10	15.30	15.30	5.10	

Cost --   R&D Product Dev.   Asset Reduction   Sales

expected financial results. These summaries will help you balance the company impact of the various programs by understanding the P&L and cash flow impact of the programs and, if necessary, make sure that the enablement is self-funding.

Macro Analysis—Manufacturing and Capital

As with the service business review, the macro analysis presents business improvement possibilities in response to the macro Web impact. A quick tabulation of possible improvements with enablement follows.

Pace

Enablement allows for real-time communication with vendors using the "pull-system" demanded by the JIT manufacturing processes. The entire order entry and fulfillment process can change as a result of the Web, which will reduce work-in-process inventory levels and overall manufacturing cycle time and effectively improve capacity without incremental capital investment. In a manufacturing environment, you need not implement an all-or-nothing order entry process because in most companies the "80-20" rule applies—that is 80 percent of the value is concentrated in 20 percent of the items. With concentrations that high, companies can "enable" a major part of their business with less investment than you might expect.

Product improvements will result from "real-time" communication about product failures in the field, linkages to suppliers, engineering functions, manufacturing, and so on. Direct wireless links from service to manufacturing will inform the operations area when systemic product problems arise—there is no need to wait for monthly or quarterly reporting. Basically, accelerate the information flow to improve performance.

Architecture

Immediate communications and an open architecture will allow feedback throughout the entire supply chain and order fulfillment cycle about product design, quality, and customer satisfaction. It is important that every facet of the manufacturing organization adhere to the open architecture policy; the Web will make the process more effective through rapid communication. Examples of an open architecture can include competitive intelligence when customers discuss competitive products that are better designed or that perform better.

If customers want special features, the Web allows for open communication and also allows for collaborative research with design, engineering, and materials experts around the globe to determine whether unique products can be manufactured and what the estimated costs, delivery times, and so forth, are. An open architecture can be an ideal source of product development if the company heeds the needs of customers.

Considering inside-out communications, a constant positive pressure to improve the business operations and Web access may encourage global marketing research of competitive products or substitute products. Using the Web, *ad hoc* research can be also "invited" using industry-specific message boards and established research Web communities to provide "outside-in" communications.

Web communications can be completely anonymous, which may encourage constituents to comment about things that otherwise would never be raised. Companies can have perpetual survey processes that query information about their products, competitive products, and customer impressions. Surveys can be summarized and analyzed and trend analysis prepared and compared against market trends.

Global

Expanded sales territory reach can be virtually anywhere in the world using the Web. In the case study, we noticed that Europe and the Far East sales were falling behind the market and historical trends and no sales were recorded in Latin America. The Web will allow research, identification, and sales through various local channels virtually anywhere on the globe. Using the Web, the company can market directly to foreign technical organizations, directly to customers, and so on. The Web also allows for online technical troubleshooting, service manuals, and promotional materials in the local language. If a company sells through local distributors that have developed translations of service and installation procedures, foreign language manuals may be available in the United States to those who are not fluent in English—for example, Spanish translations would be very helpful in the southeast and southwest. As distributors develop local materials, these may be immediately available to other common language customers—for example, Spanish translations may be very useful throughout South America and Spain.

As a caution, once these foreign territories are opened, be prepared to deal with the local requirements or define the languages and territories supported. E-commerce also makes selling small ticket items much simpler because credit cards can be preapproved for shipments and selling prices can be denominated in U.S. dollars.

Education

Education can be used for company expatriates to inform them of company policies and provide technical training, product training, and advanced functional training in areas such as selling, marketing, and planning. Approved training courses for specific topics can be completely administered through the Web by educational organizations (e.g., American Management Association, the Federal Aviation Administration). Training and record keeping over the Web is simple, often available 24 hours a day. Webinars discussing broader topics that require little interaction from the audience provide insight and training to thousands of people daily. The Web also allows for delayed playback if observers cannot attend the live performance—what excellent flexibility to learn! The Web can also be used to train distributors, customers, and organizations that may be required to service the equipment. Realistically, there is no limit to the type and extent of training that can be delivered over the Web.

Structure

Because the Web allows for global presence, using many constituents for market presence, company structure may need to change to deal with remote distributors, export sales, foreign currency exposure, and so on. Additional internal and external resources focused on these new demands may be required to develop, plan, and manage specific activities around the globe and inside and outside the company. Web consultants, legal specialists, foreign customs experts, and so forth may be required to properly deal with this expanded business. As the business expands beyond the established geography, product lines may also expand beyond the basic U.S. products through remote sourcing and regionally specific products. Because virtually every functional area may be affected by the enablement, management should evaluate the impact on the organization structure. And remember, it is not necessary to hire permanent staff to deal with the new business processes, but you may want to consider contract workers to fill temporary needs.

Summary

This chapter summarized case studies that demonstrate that the Web creates both tactical and macro advantage whether a service business or capital goods business. The case studies challenge conventional wisdom that *all or nothing* is necessary to be competitive. As we saw, a partial Web implementation will create a competitive advantage, improve performance, and provide funding for additional improvements. If companies approach e-business knowing that they can create value using the Web, programs will be identified and implemented.

We have also seen that marginal improvement in company processes will lead to significant value to the company as a result of operating leverage. In most companies, expense inputs represent 80 percent or more of sales and pretax profits represent the remainder. A simple 10 percent improvement of economic value in inputs (8 percent) represents a major improvement in profit—in this example, from 20 percent of sales to 28 percent. Small incremental steps using the Web will also create competitive advantage, once again improving profitability and shareholder value.

CHAPTER 8

MASTERING THE PLAN IMPLEMENTATION

Introduction

Mastering the plan is not an easy task because we are dealing with cultural changes, new technology, and possibly new constituents, so assume that you will meet resistance. The best methods to overcome resistance are to understand and resolve the constituent's objections, involve them in the planning phase, establish a method of governance, and properly train them for their role in enabling the company.

The team should include the formal and informal leaders in your company, the technical experts required for execution, and people with a passion for e-business. Once the structure is set and staffed, decisions will be easier to justify, make, and implement. You will find that the *open* architecture may initially appear to encourage dissent, but as the project continues, openness and candid discussion about obstacles will allow you to complete the project much more successfully.

Establish governance early and define the organization hierarchy so that participants know with whom to talk about each element of the project. Governance also means defining guidelines describing the enablement activities, communication processes, and team accountabilities. Meeting schedules, reporting processes, deadlines, and decision-making rules should be established for the entire team, including constituents outside your direct control, such as vendors, customers, and other unrelated participants.

Last, establish ongoing responsibilities for "housekeeping"—maintaining a smoothly functioning e-business company. As with all other major programs, you must *reinvent* throughout the e-business process to increase its value. Assign responsibilities to train personnel, refresh the websites, monitor the metrics, maintain a secure environment, and continually enhance the enablement process throughout the company to ensure a fully competitive value-added e-business company. If you do not establish housekeeping processes, you will be worse off than never having started the process because enablement will have become just another *temporary program of the year* rather than changing the substance of how you do business. The lack of housekeeping will expose your business to hackers and publicly display mediocrity. Exhibit 8.1

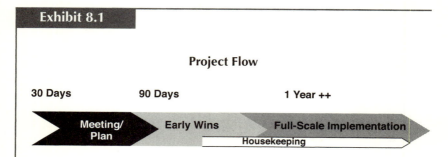

Exhibit 8.1

Project Flow

30 Days

90 Days

1 Year ++

Meeting/Plan — Early Wins — Full-Scale Implementation

Housekeeping

Broad assessment and initial plan should be completed within 30 days of enablement start. Staffing within 30 days.

Early wins will be fully implemented within the first 90 days. These are the quick projects that will generate fast returns and enthusiasm for the enablement project.

Full-scale implementation will begin at 120 days from project start and will continue for a year (plus or minus). These projects can be anywhere in the company and, depending on strategy, may be self-funding.

Housekeeping will begin early in the enablement process because there is such a fast cycle time in e-business. Website maintenance, security, and ongoing training are essential to keep the project fresh to all constituents.

demonstrates the flow of the project from the early organization meetings through full-scale implementation, which should be well under way within a year of the first meetings. Financial results and organizational change will be realized within 120 days of the start of the project.

This is a rapid implementation, but Web enabled means *speed*. A critical part of any enablement is early successes, which allow team members to enjoy a sense of accomplishment. Early wins should be implemented within 60 to 90 days of starting the project. Note that housekeeping also begins in that time frame to ensure a properly controlled and maintained enablement project.

Organization

The organization will evolve quickly through the following phases in the first month:

- Initially the chief executive officer (CEO) and the e-business executive will broadly define a tentative strategy and the team requirements. Although the strategy and team composition will not be finalized until the strategy meetings have been completed, general direction is necessary to get the project moving. The momentum of the first organization meetings will be lost if preliminary priorities are not defined by the CEO and the e-business executive early.

- Once the broad company direction is defined, identify the project executive committee (EC) or senior project leaders who will develop the business strategy. Realistically, there should be no major change in EC because this is a policy-level group of executives that will guide the company strategy. The EC should include the CEO, the e-business executive, and a selection of senior functional leaders, technology experts, and key constituents who will ensure effective e-business strategy development and execution. Companies often find it useful to have the CEO on the team to coax outside participants—vendors or customers—to participate.

Project team members will be identified by the EC based on the preliminary strategy, understanding that the final team may vary somewhat as the final strategies and priorities are developed and accepted by the EC. Select the team based on the management, functional, and technical skills required to enable the company. For example, if the initial *e-business* goals concentrate on sales operations and supply chain management, be sure that those functional leaders are on the e-business team. In most organizations, the senior functional leaders should be included in the management team that enables a company because no matter what is done, changes to company strategy may affect their function. Establishing the initial project direction and team requirements should be done in *week 1,* and initial meetings should be completed by about *week 4.*

Expect the matrix management process used in the Web enablement to be difficult to manage, even if the participants have an incentive to deliver tasks in both their primary role and this project role, and plan accordingly. Whereas internal company participants will be easy to recruit, team members from outside the company will be more difficult to enlist. Each participant will ask, "What's in it for me?" and you must be creative to develop incentives for participants to gain their commitment.

Once you have identified the preliminary organization, assess the technology gap between the expected need and the talent available to identify the training required during the initial project meetings. Team members will not be e-business experts, but we do want to have a usable base of technical expertise. In addition to defining the training requirements, this gap analysis will be the talent-recruiting checklist for final candidate selection. The organization's needs assessment should reflect the functional, technical, and managerial requirements and scheduling constraints of available personnel.

At the conclusion of the first team meetings, finalize the organization structure and select participants based on the strategy and project priorities identified, recognizing that staff selection will be an iterative process because personnel may not be available for the priorities identified. You also may need to hire consultants to supplement the existing staff.

E-business team members should be quick learners, be technologically aware, and have strong leadership traits. They should be reasonably aggressive, willing to challenge the status quo and take calculated risks, and have a history of successful project execution. Participants must be team players who can focus on the team objectives without undue consideration for their personal point of view. *Assemble the proper team, or you will not effectively enable the company.*

In addition to specific functional executives, the initial enablement team should include the following:

- The e-business leader, who will be a permanent member at the executive level. The leader will be a visionary, technologically aware, and able to integrate business strategy, technical innovations, and application priorities within the entire constituent group. The team leader must be creative, sensitive, and diplomatic to establish and manage the team.
- The technical director, who will be Web savvy, technically oriented, and able to deal with the technical challenges of the Web and the business needs of the company. This individual must envision business benefits and applications from technical activities, communicate the potential benefits and costs, and negotiate with team members to prioritize and implement processes. This should be a long-term position because this type of oversight and linkage to strategy will benefit the company.
- The e-business intelligence manager, whose role will require surveillance of competitors' activities, industry activities, and global awareness of technological advances that will improve the company competitiveness. This will be a temporary position (1 to 2 years) until the functions within the organization are e-business oriented and can be performed independently.
- The key functional leaders, who, based on the company priorities, will be appointed as needed. These selected functional experts (e.g., supply chain management, research and development [R&D], marketing) will be temporary project roles.

Compensation and Rewards

It is difficult to properly compensate team members for performance in the matrix structure required in an e-business project. Be sure to review the objectives with all team leaders, and compensate the entire team based on the successful completion of company objectives because group objectives will bond the team. The objectives should be identified for the team and each team member, and each participant's personal performance rating and overall compensation/bonus should be affected by the team goals achieved.

You must manage the outsiders (e.g., consultants, vendors, customers) differently based on their relationship with the company and the potential benefits to them. Benefits to these outside constituents should be measurable so that they can easily develop their own cost/benefit analyses—for example, customers may improve order-processing cycles, thereby reducing inventory; vendors may sell more as a result of concentrated buying for articles such as office supplies; and so on. Regardless of their role, the participants will be responsible to the project leader to perform the tasks properly.

Governance (Decision Making, Reporting, Communication, Structure)

The key to governance is the EC and the rules that they define to manage the enablement process. Governance will define how to select, approve, and manage the project components, the analytical methods and metrics (e.g., return on investment, return on assets, annual cash flow requirements), and team and team member responsibilities. Once the governance is established, there should be no ambiguity as to how the project will be managed. Some common elements of governance include organization structure and composition, mission, communication, and decision-making rules.

Organization was discussed earlier and will include a preliminary and a final structure and composition. Unfortunately, a two-step approach to defining the organization may be necessary because the final strategy will not be determined until after the first enablement meetings.

The *mission* statement defines the purpose of the project. The CEO/ e-business leader should develop a preliminary mission statement to guide the team and to organize the projects, understanding that the mission statement may be modified based on the organization's input. The mission should be broad enough to be long lasting—probably more than 1 year— but specific enough to be a basis for decision making and prioritizing projects during a planning period. Without a mission statement, the project may be unfocused and may flounder rather than accomplish specific company objectives. An example mission statement follows:

> *The e-business* mission is to lead, coordinate, and support e-business activities. *The e-business team will coordinate the e-business strategy by assembling key business leaders and providing basic technology training and a summary of company business issues. The* team will prioritize e-business initiatives *and identify the organization structure and project leaders to execute the e-business programs at periodic strategy meetings. Project leaders and participants will be individuals and/or organizations that can successfully implement the programs, and they may be outside the company. The e-business team will support the initiatives throughout their identification, implementation, and future maintenance requirements. Responsibilities may shift among the constituents to ensure that, on an ongoing basis, all applications are effectively maintained and refreshed to meet or exceed competitive requirements. The* e-business executive will lead the e-business *initiative to enable the company and will prioritize the projects within the overall budget developed by the e-business team. All e-business development must be coordinated through the e-business leader to avoid a fragmented company effort, which may result in a disparate "look and feel" to both internal and external constituents.*

The executive committee should define decision-making rules and policy statements about decision authority, approval levels, and types of decisions that can be made. Analyses and metrics that will be used for the decision process, such as return on investment, sales or profit increases, cash flow impact, and so forth, can be outlined in a standard format. The EC should also approve major deviations from project deliverables, spending, and major changes in organization. As necessary, the e-business leader and the EC will reemphasize the project priority, change business priorities, and change resources allocated to the project. Exhibit 8.2 shows an approvals matrix that covers personnel, expense, and asset spending approvals' levels within the organization.

Once the overall enablement plan is approved, many individual decisions can be executed without further approval, which will accelerate the implementation plan. The approval matrix is defined according to level in the "e-business team" rather than organization level in the company because some team members may be outside the company. *Communication processes,* including both formal and informal channels, must be two-way (inbound or listening) and outbound. Communications include broad communications such as newsletters and more formal, focused communications such as project status reports for the entire project or segments thereof. Communication

Exhibit 8.2

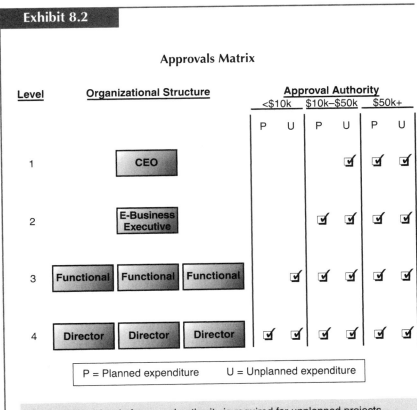

Approvals Matrix

Level	Organizational Structure	Approval Authority <$10k		$10k–$50k		$50k+	
		P	U	P	U	P	U
1	CEO				☑	☑	☑
2	E-Business Executive			☑	☑	☑	☑
3	Functional Functional Functional		☑	☑	☑	☑	☑
4	Director Director Director	☑	☑	☑	☑	☑	☑

P = Planned expenditure   U = Unplanned expenditure

Note: A higher level of approval authority is required for unplanned projects. Also, a monthly financial review is required for project to date and projected cost to completion.

requirements will be defined in the organization meetings and will establish the elements of routine communications and exception reporting. A structured communication process eliminates confusion and also ensures that significant issues are properly identified and resolved. Communication is not just outward from the task force but also inward from virtually any source because the open architecture requires that management encourages and accepts inbound communication. Many enablement projects use a *Web page* as a bulletin board for the open communications.

A periodic newsletter is a useful way to communicate with participants. Editorials celebrating early wins and publicly reinforcing project goals or encouraging the teams to continue their work are excellent tools. A newsletter also informs the outside constituents about project progress, but remember that once you publish information, the information could be shared with competitors, government agencies, and so forth. If you do not have effective inbound and outbound communications, the Web enablement project will fail.

Simulated Application

Meetings

The first and the most important meeting of the enablement team is the introduction to the project. This meeting will include a discussion of the mission and strategy, a brief technology session, brainstorming of potential applications that may be applicable to the company strategy development, and project assessment and prioritization. At the conclusion of the meeting, the team leaders will understand the goals, timetables, business risks/opportunities, and technology that may be useful to them in the future. The organization and governance will be reviewed to ensure that there is a clear understanding of who is on the project and how the project will be managed. At the completion of the first organization meeting, the macro strategy will be complete and the detailed planning may begin, initially with the highest-level project, then moving progressively down through more narrowly defined tasks that accomplish the overall strategy. As the high-level projects are defined, the team should validate the expected financial impact—both spending and savings—and determine whether the projects actually make sense.

Ongoing meeting schedules will include both formal monthly *executive review* sessions to ensure that the entire project is on schedule and team *work sessions* to get the job done. It will not be easy to schedule these meetings unless the enablement process is a priority for the constituents, so be sure to schedule reporting based on the priority of the deliverable and the risk to the project. *Once you establish the detailed e-business plan, organization, and governance, the project will nearly manage itself.* If you do not finalize the plan, organization, and governance, enablement will flounder. Once you start the enablement, be prepared to adjust the schedule components, reallocate resources, and modify some of the interim priorities.

The initial organization meeting will require 1 to 2 days and include the following agenda items:

- Organization structure and participation
- Mission
- Governance
- Introduction to technology

- Success stories
- Break-out session for brainstorming opportunity
- Strategy
- Selection of priority projects

Introduction to Technology

Before we can identify the technology and the training requirements, we must understand the company strategy. The CEO should broadly define the strategic vision before the meeting, knowing that the final strategy will be developed by the end of the meeting. For example, if the strategy were to expand European products, sell over the Web to European Economic Community (EEC) countries, and service the products offshore, we would need trained resources who understand the European marketing requirements. European sales and service may require expertise in video conferencing, remote product design capabilities, specialized project management software, and so forth. In this example, Web technology and EEC tax, legal, and financing expertise will be required because we expect to sell over the Web. If we choose to use distributors for remote European locations, we may need experts to help us develop the requirements for such remote distribution.

The technology session will fill the knowledge gap that we identified earlier as we reviewed the organization, train people in the basics of Web enablement, and also introduce the team to some advanced concepts, success stories, and applications. The introduction to technology should be brief but sufficient to begin the enablement process. Once the participants understand the potential impact of enablement, they will chart their own course of learning. As participants relate newly learned technical capabilities and their functional knowledge and desire for value improvement, they will develop a selection of strategy alternatives.

It is better to have too many knowledge experts available at the initial meeting than not enough. Although a final strategy has not yet been defined, the CEO and e-business leaders should define the broad topical areas in anticipation of their prioritization. Examples of technology that may provide some immediate benefits include the following:

- Voice-Over Internet Protocol (VOIP)—technology
- Customer relationship management (CRM)—technology
- Supply chain management—purchasing
- Wireless—technology
- Web conferencing—technology

VOIP will provide immediate long-distance savings to almost any company, and supply chain management usually reduces costs immediately. The benefits of some of the other technologies are more dependent on the company's competitive condition.

Success Stories

Presenting and discussing Web success stories from other companies in similar industries will also energize the participants. Quite often, executives who have successfully ventured into new processes are proud of their accomplishments and are anxious to share their experience with other companies. If the executives are not available to travel, use a WebEx conference call to both experience the video conferencing technology and hear the success story. Success stories give tangible evidence of the benefits of enablement and also allow team members to talk about the challenges that were overcome during the process. Face-to-face communication is an excellent way to build credibility for enablement.

Break-Out Sessions

During the break-out sessions, groups of executives will identify possible applications, estimated timelines for implementation, benefits, and costs. During these meetings, be careful not to adopt an *all-or-nothing* attitude, which will result in missed opportunities—for example, executives who are concerned that the company cannot implement a purchasing program may miss an easy opportunity to apply an "Office Products" application. Also, you might consider a low-cost pilot project that will allow you to test assumptions and clarify costs and benefits while keeping costs low, giving you an opportunity to determine whether the change makes sense. The CEO and e-business leader should challenge the groups to analyze specific value-added opportunities. The break-out group leader should review the results of these smaller meetings with all meeting attendees.

Strategy

The enablement strategy will be developed based on several factors, such as the business opportunities and current market position, technology, and fiscal constraints. The strategy will be a template that describes specific long-range objectives so that in the near term, the organization is not continually disrupted with changes in direction. The strategy will define what, when, where, how, and who will be enabled and will guide the entire team to select the best projects. An example enablement strategy might be as follows:

The Web-enablement strategy will reduce the overall selling general and administrative (SG&A) costs to less than 35 percent of sales using Web processes. Initial priorities will focus early wins *in any area, to fund overall enablement strategies; on* sales and marketing *functions, which directly support the customer; and also the* manufacturing and supply chain, *to improve quality, cost, and service to the customer. Improvements in administrative service activities will be a secondary priority. Incremental sales growth of 5 percent more than market growth will be achieved through* territory and channel expansion of existing products and through incremental service revenues. *Funding of the initiatives will be* cost neutral on an annual basis *initially and* additive to earnings by year 3. *Capital investments to support the enablement process may be as high as 5 percent of annual capital expenditures. Net earnings as a percent of sales will increase from 8 percent to 10 percent by the end of the planning period.*

Measurable goals and specific guidelines provide a framework for decision making. For example, if the company chooses to expand its existing product sales to Europe, it is acceptable as a territory expansion; however, if the company chooses to develop new products for the 220V European market, it would be a departure from the existing product line and outside the scope of the strategy.

Detailed Plan

We should first identify and implement some significant early wins to fund enablement for the entire company and show that enablement works. Quite often, these would begin with purchasing, telecom, travel, training, and perhaps space planning for those few high-growth organizations that exist in today's economy.

Exhibit 8.3 shows a listing of projects in a company's e-business plan. The exhibit includes a project description, an individual responsible for the project, a timeline, and the value to the company. Value helps focus attention on the priority projects, often based on profits. A simple summary will allow better communication with team members and other interested parties.

The information included on the summary page is a brief summary of individual worksheets that will be prepared for each project. Exhibit 8.4 shows a more detailed worksheet that will be prepared for each project

Exhibit 8.3

Company E-Business Plan

Project #	Resp.	Description	Quarter 1	2	3	4	Value (Millions $)	Quarter 1	2	3	4	Value (Millions $)	Cumulative
1	IT	**VOIP telecom system**					+0.2					+0.5	+0.7
2	Purchasing	**Implement PSP purchasing—initial** Travel, Office Supplies, MRO					+1.1					+1.5	+2.6
3	Purchasing	**Implement PSP secondary** Manufacturing material; assembly/subassembly					+1.1					+1.7	+2.8
4	IT	**Web conferencing; training**					+1.1					+2.1	+3.2
5	Sales	**CRM implementation**					+0.4					+2.4	+2.8
6	Service	**Service manuals—online**					−0.4					+0.7	+0.3
7	Admin.	**Virtual office**					−0.4					+1.0	+0.6
8	R&D	**R&D collaboration**					−0.5					+1.0	+0.5
9	Marketing	**Expand global marketing**										−2.5	−2.5
		Annual Benefit					+2.6					+11.9	
		Cumulative Benefit					+2.6					+14.5	+14.5

Exhibit 8.4

Project Justification Worksheet—VOIP

Description

Implement VOIP to eliminate long-distance charges and improve phone connectivity. Project will be completed within 90 days. No downtime. No changes to sales or office training required to implement.

Timeline

	Outlay					
1	2	3	4	5	6	7

	Outlay		Savings	Probability Annual	Weighted Savings	DCF	Cumulative	Net Cash Flow
	Annual	Cumulative						
Assets								
Server	$25	$25						
Software	$15	$15						
Total	**$40**	**$40**						

Head count
N/A—Additional tasks for IT department are minimal. No change in head count.

Expenses		Savings	Probability Annual	Weighted Savings
Long-distance charges		$35	100%	$35

Notes:

Project payback is less than 18 months. Discounted cash flow (DFC) unnecessary.
Additional features such as video conferencing will be more practical as a result of this project.

accepted by the EC. Although the specific elements of the worksheets may vary among companies, several elements should be included in all worksheets, as follows:

- The *project description* describes the project in enough detail that it can be managed. Details should include equipment type, software vendors, and roughly what is expected when the project is fully implemented. A brief timeline shows approximate implementation schedule, but a more detailed project implementation schedule must be prepared to effectively manage the project.
- *Costs and benefits* (in this case, subdivided into capital and expense) are important because of the impact on return on assets and the annual profit and loss (P&L) impact. The example also includes head count, which may be important in some investment decisions.
- A *Notes section* is available to describe any other features that may be important to discussing the project. In some cases, the project itself may not result in any immediate benefits but will improve the infrastructure and be a foundation for further Web-enablement enhancements.

Exhibit 8.4 is an example template that can be used to evaluate and manage specific applications. It shows an evaluation of VOIP, which requires no initial capital outlay but does require a 3-year operating lease. The operating lease covers the software and hardware required to activate VOIP, which performs all the telecommunication's functions. With these initial purchases and minor maintenance upgrades, long-distance and local calling, conference calls, video conferencing, voice mail, caller ID, and remote access are available for minimal routine cost. Savings can be significant; Grant Thornton (a major international audit firm) estimates that the net annual savings for their VOIP installation totals about $800,000.[45]

Cost savings achieved by purchasing applications for companies not yet Web enabled are generally realized simply because of the competitive bidding and order consolidation capabilities of the Web. There are several ways to approach purchasing:

- Use an applications systems provider (ASP) to purchase some of the primary commodities that are used by the company. These could be organizations centered on a particular vertical market—hospital

---

[45] "On Site; Grant Thornton LLP and Avaya VOIP: Creating Conversations Among 2,700 People in 44 Locations," by The Aberdeen Group, June 2002, http://www.aberdeen.com.

supplies, steel, electronic components, and so on—that can afford group-purchasing volumes not otherwise achievable by the company.

- Concentrate volumes of like components to receive volume discounts and other benefits from leverage on vendors. In many cases, concentrating office supplies' purchases with a single vendor may save *10 to 15 percent.* Order cycle times and administrative costs will be improved whenever you use Web-based purchasing. Web-based travel services often save 30 to 40 percent of cost.
- Establish a policy that in-house training will be used immediately for functional training, and, for example, service and repair training. This will save considerable time and travel cost.
- Substantially reduce telecom charges by using VOIP either through an ASP or through company-owned facilities.
- Implement CRM software, such as that available from Salesforce.com. Use of such software will realize early benefits if sales closing rates are improved. Implementation of the CRM and ASP will be quick and effective and provide immediate benefit.
- Collaborate on R&D to substantially reduce travel costs and time committed to collaborate. Once again, ASPs like WebEx can save you thousands of dollars. A quick tabulation of some of the savings is included in Exhibit 8.5.

Once these quick hits are harvested, more substantive, strategic programs can be developed and implemented.

Exhibit 8.5

Average Benefits of Procurement Outsourcing

Description	Improvement
Price reductions	15–25%
Contract compliance	55–65%
Reduced administrative costs	25–35%
Head count reduction	15–20%
Faster procurement cycles	27–55%
Reduced procurement automation costs	25–30%

Source: Adapted from "The Procurement Outsourcing Benchmark Report, Accelerating and Sustaining Total Cost Savings," by The Aberdeen Group, March 2004, p. 16.

Exhibit 8.6

Housekeeping—Planning

	Responsibility	Frequency				
		Daily	Weekly	Monthly	Quarterly	Annually
Hardware Systems						
Servers		✓			✓	✓
Communications					✓	
BlackBerry	IT			✓		
Cellular	Telecom			✓		
Wireless	Telecom			✓		
VOIP	IT			✓		
Conference video	IT			✓		
Remote access	IT			✓	✓	
Laptops				✓		✓
Wireless	IT			✓	✓	
Conference video	IT					
Training	IT			✓	✓	✓
Software Systems						
VOIP	IT			✓		✓
Conferencing	IT				✓	
Security						
Software upgrades	IT	✓		✓	✓	✓
Failures/follow-up	IT	✓	✓	✓	✓	✓
Training	IT			✓	✓	✓
Content						
Functional departments						
Marketing	Marketing	✓	✓			
Regulatory	Reg			✓	✓	
Consumer awareness	Consumer Affairs			✓	✓	
Finance	Finance			✓	✓	
Legal	Legal			✓	✓	
Sales—Web	Sales Operations	✓	✓	✓		
Sales—Web	Sales Mgmt.				✓	✓
Frequently asked questions	All	✓				
Consumer complaints	Consumer Affairs	✓		✓	✓	✓
Web pages						
Home	All			✓		
Financial information	Finance			✓	✓	✓
Product help function	Prod. Development			✓		
Other sites—cross-reference				✓		
Department of Labor	HR			✓		
Department of Health, Education, and Welfare	HR		✓			
Training	All			✓	✓	✓

Housekeeping

Early in this chapter, we reviewed a rough implementation plan in Exhibit 8.1, which includes *housekeeping* starting at about 90 days into the program. Housekeeping, which will be discussed further in Chapter 10, means maintaining a properly managed Web environment. The elements that are affected by the Web should be examined to establish the ongoing requirements and can be summarized as hardware, software, or personnel requirements. In Exhibit 8.6, several of the elements are listed. The summary reflects hardware, software, and content. Define what is most important to your company. This summary represents the most important features of the applications, as well as a scheduled review or information refreshment. The summary includes both responsibility and frequency. The best way to consider housekeeping is to remember that the Web is real-time, and everything that you do on the Web is exposed to your current and potential employees, customers, vendors, competitors, and anyone else who may have an interest in your company (e.g., potential and current investors, retirees, governments). The housekeeping checklist will make sure that you have the best presentation while managing the costs.

Establish a review cycle for assessment and preventive maintenance for each element of the housekeeping responsibility based on the business risk to the systems/processes, total benefit, and costs. The presentation and activities performed must always be correct and fresh to the users in the instant Web environment. Few factors create such a negative image for a Web-enabled company than a website that does not work properly or contains outdated information. The website and Web activities are a window to your business proficiency.

Summary

In this and the last seven chapters, we have discussed the business environment, which can be very hostile, yet very lucrative, for any business. When you manage the environment well, you will harvest significant benefits and be more competitive. This chapter discussed how you make the enablement happen and develop and manage the process in your particular company. The only factors left for a successful application are locating all the sources of enablement and specifically defining your housekeeping processes. These will be relatively short chapters because the work is real-time and process oriented, rather than descriptive of the sources that will be used. Because the Web is real-time, once this book is published, the sources of enablement will be outdated. However, the processes described to become enabled will not be outdated. Chapter 9 will discuss the processes to be used to stay current in enablement technology and applications, and Chapter 10 will briefly discuss housekeeping in a bit more detail than we have in this chapter.

Chapter 9

Assessing Available E-Commerce Resources

Introduction

We have seen many examples of how the Web can improve a business in both the short and long term. One constant throughout the discussion is that every person must be relentless in his or her pursuit of enablement because the Web is a real-time phenomenon on which everything that you do, or do not do, is subject to complete exposure to constituents. An effectively enabled company will encourage all who deal with the company—either inside or outside—to improve the interaction. No books can provide a current and all-inclusive list of all the software and hardware available to enable a company because the Web is a real-time opportunity. By the time a book is published, the specific Web references may already be outdated. People should be empowered, and the organization and all constituents must be open to change. These are not easy attributes to instill in organizations, but the people must adapt to enable the organization.

Although employees should be constantly searching for business improvements, only time, training, and reinforcement will make them proficient. Recall that the organization described in Chapter 8 included a technical director and an intelligence manager who monitored websites and identified technology improvements for applications. The intelligence manager would be necessary for only 1 to 2 years because by then employees should be responsible for that role. In this chapter, we will discuss a research method that will identify applications to be used in a company.

Once we establish the research method, we will examine several types of activities that can be enabled, and then we will identify specific applications already in use by many companies. It is important to catalog the successful applications already used to improve the likelihood of successful application in our company. The research methods will work well in both small and large companies if the communication process is simple and open. If your company is large, be sure your research process encourages and manages the flow of information. In many cases, small companies have an advantage because there are fewer layers.

The Web is not a technology but a business improvement process that could potentially involve every employee. Do not assign responsibility for finding business solutions and monitoring Web activities to just the information technology (IT) department—every employee is responsible.

Process to Identify Web Applications

Who Is Responsible?

Everyone is responsible for process improvement in a Web-enabled company—the phone operator, the secretary, the sales representative, and even the chief executive officer (CEO). The organization should empower these individuals to identify possible improvement and communicate the idea so that it can be evaluated. How many interactions and observations does an individual make every day? Since the Web is a real-time activity, ideas become outdated very quickly and business cycle times are much shorter than 10 years ago. New companies spring to the market daily with improved services or products. As a result, the best sources of information about improvements are also real-time sources, and the best method to identify the improvements on a real-time basis is to empower more observers and create a process for them to report their ideas.

Exhibit 9.1 depicts the differences between Web-enabled communication and the traditional linear forms. E-business information is unrestricted and perhaps random because communication channels are not rigidly applied. Each globe in the exhibit represents a group of constituents, and each arrow represents communication. In any particular time frame, people intersect and exchange information, as depicted by the gray arrows. The information wanders throughout the organization, continually generating new observations and conclusions. Circles of influence, such as partners and current vendors, can openly communicate to create value. Compare that with the minimal, controlled communications represented in the traditional model—linear, programmed, and not dynamic. The e-business communication model encourages problem solving and will identify more ideas if properly managed.

Encourage everyone in your company to search for improvements to your Web enablement. Use the daily interactions that your workforce has with vendors, peers, customers, and competitors as they order or sell products to do the research.

If each day an employee talks on the phone with customers or vendors for 1 hour, that employee may find improvements in the way that calls are

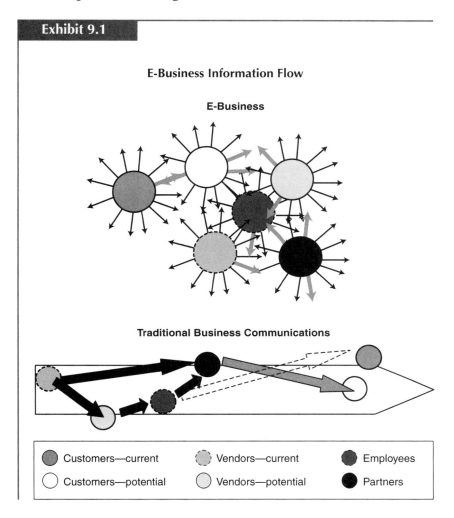

Exhibit 9.1

E-Business Information Flow

E-Business

Traditional Business Communications

| ● Customers—current | ⦿ Vendors—current | ● Employees |
| ○ Customers—potential | ◐ Vendors—potential | ● Partners |

handled. For example, customer relationship management (CRM) software, such as that available from Salesforce.com, captures all interactions with contacts for future and expanded access by authorized personnel. Has an employee ordered products from Dell recently? What better place than Dell to do the real-time market research to find the best process? Dell is perhaps one of the best Web-enabled companies in the world, for both products and services. In addition to direct selling over the Web, they also provide technical service, software upgrades, and technical troubleshooting advice over the Web. Their profit margins increase rapidly beyond basic computer margins when they offer you a discounted larger hard drive, a 3-year service contract, or additional software over the Web.

What happens when everyone is responsible and empowered to enable? Earlier in the book, we discussed the impact of 5 percent improvement in any daily activity. What if we could improve realized pricing by 1 percent using the Web? Exhibit 9.2 shows the major profit impact of such small incremental improvements.

If every employee is trained to observe and improve work performance, company earnings will increase by 45 percent in this example. Company executives are responsible for creating a continuous improvement environment in which people at any level feel responsible to improve the company performance. The regularly scheduled Web-enablement meetings, routine communications with employees, and celebrations that recognize successful applications will do just that.

Customers can also be enlisted in the Web-enablement process if you remember to tell customers what's in it for them. Your organization should ask, "How can we make it worthwhile for our customers?" Something as simple as an e-mail notification of a scheduled delivery time may be very useful for your customers. Customers may be able to schedule deliveries over the Web. Have you also considered that customers may forget about routine maintenance activities that will be required of your equipment? Each employee should challenge the customers to identify ways to improve the relationship using Web-enablement tools that already exist. As employees become more creative, more enablement improvements will be developed.

All constituents—whether vendors, competitors, consultants, or companies in similar or different industries—are sources of information for your company. Observe their Web-enablement activities and challenge your employees to improve. Service providers may change the company value chain using the Web. For example, UPS and FedEx now perform extensive logistics functions, rather than just package delivery, to improve your company performance. They can now track deliveries anywhere on the globe using the Web, and they also provide a predictable and reliable supply chain to your most demanding customers. Consider how the enabled service will provide a competitive advantage for you. Or worse, what if your competitor hires them before you do? How much money will be saved by reducing late performance fees, lost inventory, product shortages, and so on, as a result of using their services?

If your employees are trained to observe and adapt new ideas, the world is your research laboratory.

Exhibit 9.2

Average Company Profit and Loss

(Millions $)	Baseline	Resources	Marginal Improvement	
			5%	10%

Amount of Improvement

	Baseline	Resources
Sales	**100.0**	
Cost of Sales	50.0	50.0
Selling, General, & Administration		
Selling & Marketing	15.0	15.0
R&D	8.0	8.0
Administration—Finance, HR, IT, Legal	15.0	15.0
All Other	2.0	2.0
Total Costs	**90.0**	**90.0**
Pretax Profit	**10.0**	
Improved Profit @ 5% Improvement		14.5
Improved Profit @ 10% Improvement		19.0

*

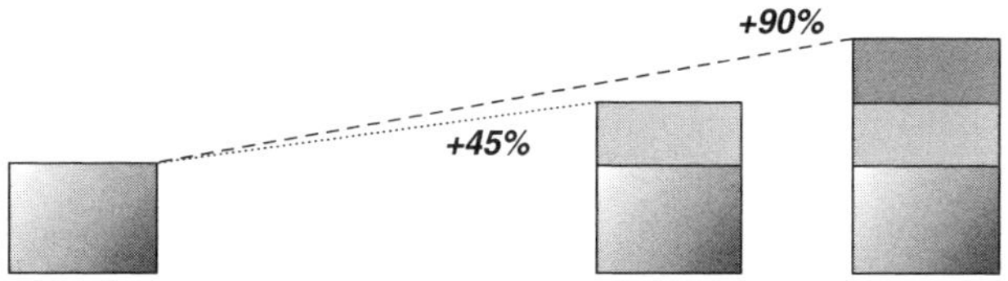

+45%

+90%

Marginal improvements add up to big profit increases.

Professional Organizations

In addition to the normal workday activities and observations, encourage employees to join professional organizations that discuss functions, industries, and technologies at monthly meetings and periodic national conferences. How often have you attended a meeting and identified a potential opportunity that could be used by your company, but you had no process to communicate the idea? How many people attend these activities, and what do you gain as a result of their attendance? When a subordinate attends a conference, require that they prepare a summary of key conference points to share with the company.

Attend a professional meeting for your specialty or another functional area to expand your thinking—the chief financial officer (CFO) may attend the National Association of Marketing Executives meeting to understand another perspective. There is no limit to creativity once the *smokestack* mentality is eliminated and people focus on delivering value to the company. When a Web-enablement problem is solved, executives are no longer crossing division or functional lines.

Reading

Of course Web improvements can be found in *Wired Magazine* and *CIO Magazine,* but improvements can also be found in *Fortune, Business Week, Forbes, Sports Illustrated, Ski Magazine, Yachting,* and so forth. Rather than searching for technology in the media, you should be searching for e-business improvement using technology. Think about some of the articles and advertisements that you have seen in these nonbusiness magazines and how you can adapt the innovation to your company. Do your employees read magazines, promotional information, and newspapers? Each is a source of improvement on a real-time basis.

Peer Groups

Divisions or business units in larger companies may identify and implement solutions that are not shared with others in the company. If you are in a large company, how often do you discuss e-business or your function with peers in other divisions? What if they have discovered an e-business solution that you have not yet used? Remove the barriers and focus on finding e-business improvements.

Competitors

In the last chapter, we identified a job responsibility for an e-business intelligence manager who observed the e-business market—for example, monitoring competitive websites. In a real-time world, can you afford to be 6 months behind your competitor? Competitors may use a website for pilot projects, which will give you an advance warning of certain development activities. Do they now sell and service in an expanded geography? Do they have a Spanish language section? Do they have service manuals on the Web? If yes, do you have an opportunity for product research in addition to understanding how they sell? Do they have their pricing information on the Web? The e-business intelligence manager will monitor Web applications to understand and inform the executive committee (EC) of Web-enablement activities. Each functional area may also assign representatives to monitor competitive sites for improvement because you may find Web improvement in totally different industries.

Similar Industries

Do not be restricted to observing a single industry. Have you considered using Webinars in consumer products, service, or capital goods industries? Service training films are available on a real-time, downloadable basis for service technicians or even individual consumers. Think outside the lines and adapt successful applications to your business.

Kinds of Applications

All companies have a unique value chain that defines their competitive position. As you assess possible applications, focus on the elements of the value chain that are most important to your business. Exhibit 9.3 lists the primary and secondary activities of the value chain of any business, some of which are more important than others. Select the elements within your chain that will gain the most benefit from enablement, and examine those functional areas in other businesses.

Summary of Activities

Activities should be viewed in the same creative way by all personnel. The question "Is there a better way?" must be answered, and what better people to answer the question than those who actually perform the task. Empower

Exhibit 9.3

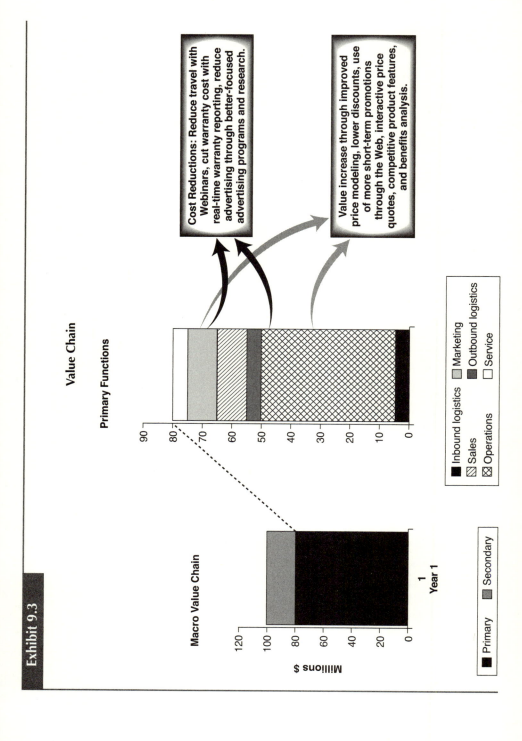

Value Chain

Primary Functions

Cost Reductions: Reduce travel with Webinars, cut warranty cost with real-time warranty reporting, reduce advertising through better-focused advertising programs and research.

Value increase through improved price modeling, lower discounts, use of more short-term promotions through the Web, interactive price quotes, competitive product features, and benefits analysis.

■ Inbound logistics   ■ Marketing
▨ Sales   ■ Outbound logistics
⊠ Operations   □ Service

Macro Value Chain

Millions $

Year 1

■ Primary   ■ Secondary

the employees to use their imaginations, contacts, and observations to improve processes. Employees may observe e-business activities at their favorite music retailer, their favorite jewelry store, or the local car dealership. Adapt the processes to be successful.

In an earlier chapter we listed the activities performed. Now use the open-minded and well-informed employees to first challenge the need to perform the activity and then challenge the way in which it is performed considering the Web processes. Although the checklist in Exhibit 9.4 can be prepared centrally by the e-business team, push the responsibility down through the organization to make every employee responsible to improve the business using e-business techniques. Many contributors will improve the likelihood of success. It is not just a *big* idea that creates value, but many small ideas that will improve firm value and profitability. A key to the wholehearted support of the e-business infrastructure is smart business. Whenever possible look for what additional activities can be done in the market (e.g., improving shipping processes, new product training) rather than how to decrease cost. A brief list of activities that will improve e-business follows:

- *Communications:* Using the Web can dramatically reduce the cost of business. Inexpensive Voice-Over Internet Protocol (VOIP) can improve the level of service by having remote access and close linkage to the CRM software.
- *Training:* Using video conferencing, sites such as WebEx, or streaming video allows you to train personnel virtually anywhere. With today's inexpensive video conferencing technology, it is possible to have direct video conferencing with anyone, anywhere, anytime. Whereas historically a company was limited to a large investment or to commercial sites such as Kinko's, inexpensive hardware, software technology, and broadband access have made video conferencing affordable to almost anyone. Many of the presentations can be stored online for indefinite periods, making them accessible for viewing almost anytime. Consider the impact of step-by-step training for offsite service representatives. Training at home will save travel time (lost billable hours) and also allow for employees to schedule training at their leisure. Training can be expanded beyond anything considered reasonable before because accessibility is no longer as time or money intense as before.
- *Research:* Research activities can be expanded to new organizations never before considered—universities and government organizations

Exhibit 9.4

Activities Analysis

Product: photocopier

Marketing Function	Today	Future
Market Research		
Geographic expansion	Personal calls; sales rep/distributor network input by phone and paper.	Web research for regional distributors; direct e-mail followed by phone and personal visits.
Competitive Analysis		
Local news	Empower local employees to identify competitive information published.	Review all local business journals for new companies: contracts and RFPs, changes in executives; set up Web agents to search for news.
National news	Empower employees to identify competitive information published and "heard on the street."	Review all national business news for competitive info: RFPs, product improvements, potential JVs and affiliations; set up Web agents to search for news.
International news	Empower employees to identify competitive information published and "heard on the street."	
Executives	Empower employees to identify executive information published and "heard on the street."	Set up Web agents to monitor specific executive's activities: promotions, transfers, presentations, etc.
Website	N/A before the Web.	Monitor competitors' websites to identify promotions, new products, innovations, new contracts, customers, product recalls, and other issues.
Message boards	N/A before the Web.	Monitor message boards to identify customer feedback, employee feedback, trends, etc.
Blogs	N/A before the Web.	Monitor employee and major customer blogs.

Marketing Function	Today	Future
Product Research		
Europe	Review patent registers printed weekly.	Monitor website regarding patents issued by EEC that may be useful in technology. Also monitor patents obtained by chief competitors.
U.S.	Review patent registers printed weekly.	Monitor website regarding patents issued by U.S. patent office that may be useful in technology. Also monitor patents obtained by chief competitors.
Universities	Review periodic paper newsletters issued.	Closely monitor website—coordinate/monitor papers published by research universities in related fields. Assign to specific researchers.
Pricing Analysis	Obtain copies/fax of promotional material issued, using sales force as source.	Scan competitive websites to monitor promotions, special pricing, etc., to identify market trends.
Product Training	Annual; paper manuals cumbersome and difficult to coordinate. Little follow-up training because of costs.	Interactive, real-time, and through Webinars. Available anytime on the Web; automated recordkeeping of testing results. Refresher courses available throughout the year.
New Product Launch	Major investment in travel for regional conferences; product rolled out over 90 days; no significant launch activity for minor product upgrades; paper manuals and CD-ROMs.	Simultaneous national launch using Webinars, coordinated interactive technical and customer training; real-time video "help desk"; minor product enhancements through Webinars; interactive training throughout the year.

191

in other countries such as Russia, Poland, China, and India—and can be real-time, interactive, and expanded well beyond the basic research completed historically. Research projects can now be collaborative, whereas before collaboration was impractical.

- *Business, legal, and patent information:* Business, legal, and patent information is now immediately accessible when authorized on databases. Competitive research and market analysis can now be fast and include information never before accessible on short notice. A review of a competitor's website may reveal company information that historically could be obtained only through extensive research of public documents. All Securities and Exchange Commission (SEC) documents are now available to anyone with Web access. Local legal documents identifying land/building transactions, permits for expansion, Environmental Protection Agency (EPA) approvals, liens, and so on, are often available online.

- *Customer feedback:* Customer feedback can be obtained in real time as well, and it can be anonymous or attributable to specific clients. Real-time information can be used to change the way you do business—using, for example, a pilot project that can be monitored today rather than waiting weeks to accumulate and analyze customer feedback. Pilot projects can now be targeted and analyzed more quickly, reducing product development cycle time. Do not think only of accelerating the process, but change how you think! Once the people are indoctrinated into e-business, many minds will search for that better way of doing business.

- *Transaction processing:* Transaction processing on the Web can reduce errors, improve order fulfillment time, reduce inventories, improve cash flow, reduce processing costs, and so on. The challenge is to determine the type of transaction processing needed to improve. Can this include something as simple as warranty registrations, in themselves of little direct profitability? When coupled with regional sales statistics, historical purchase patterns, and so forth, a company may be able to develop new marketing programs to improve its profit yield.

Examples of Web Enablement

Sales in many companies have been expanded through broader channels and geographic distribution. Sales through the Web can also smooth a business cycle to create value by using a promotional model to manage orders.

Price Modeling   Pricing modeling has improved profits dramatically when coupled with real-time ordering. Perhaps the best example of this modeling is the airline/car rental pricing that we encounter daily. Best ticket pricing can vary by as much as 10 to 15 percent within hours. Many companies can use this price modeling to manage their ultimate profitability when orders are processed in real time either directly or over the Web.

Bundling   Product bundling is handled well by companies such as Amazon and Dell, but others use the bundling for many online activities. Think about the travel industry that leads you from website reservation to other areas—airlines, to hotels, to rental cars, to local attractions.

Products offered can be better managed through real-time processing. Linkages with other sites supported by modest commissions or referral fees are now a common practice for many websites. There is little or no incremental cost for the site offering their "space" when a site is reviewed or an order is processed, but there is an upside to revenue and profit.

Purchases   Of course the range of savings related to purchased materials and supplies has been discussed extensively already. As we look at the Web, however, it is possible to create additional value in the value chain by using the Web to extend services never before offered through a channel that has previously not been available. Changing the value stream does not mean that you must terminate people; rather, it means that you may have found a better way of doing the task, and you can improve your competitiveness. As mentioned earlier, using UPS or FedEx does not necessarily mean staff reduction, but it may give a company additional capacity without additional head count.

The selling function relies heavily on information to improve the competitive position. Databases on Yahoo!, AOL, and Google can be accessed to identify industry trends, individual company activities, and even key company employees. CRM software allows the sales force to focus efforts better than before by knowing what, when, how, and to whom activities have occurred at *existing and potential customers.* Real-time presentations to customers with current information about the competitive products, real-time price quotes (e.g., sensitivity to volumes, shipping deadlines, product groupings), and special discounts available only to certain classes of customers will present a more competitive posture.

Rather than thinking of communication in a linear way, think of how the activity can be best used in the company. Sales training and video conferencing may be a perfect way to keep the sales representatives on the street rather than in offices for sales training.

Once again creativity is important.

Summary

It is important to realize that virtually anything can be improved using the Web. The real advantage will be gained when you have empowered the organization to search for, identify, and submit ideas that will capitalize on the technology. The empowerment can be beyond your employees and should include customers, vendors, and all constituents that may interact with you in the business. Never cut off the information flow, but do control the implementation process. Anything can be done on the Web!

The advantage of the Web is that you will be using the creativity of many and not just those under your direct control. Manage the process, and you will be amazed at how quickly you will become enabled. If you cooperate with the constituent base well, you will have a virtually unlimited supply of high-quality ideas for improving your business. It is important that you beat the competition to the use of the Web, so enable as soon as possible. The minds of many versus the minds of a few will create value in your company, or vice versa, for your competitors. Which would you prefer?

## CHAPTER 10

E-BUSINESS HOUSEKEEPING

Introduction

In the past chapters, we have discussed the competitive and financial opportunities that are available by enabling your company. Now that we have invested the time necessary to assess, plan, and implement e-business applications, we will define the next steps in the continuous e-business process.

E-business is your business showcase to customers, competitors, and all constituents anywhere in the world. True, you can implement a state-of-the-art website and encourage all company personnel, vendors, and customers to use the e-business applications that you have implemented, but just as the global competition does not remain stagnant, you must adapt to the continuous change and continually upgrade your processes to remain competitive. The only question that remains is "Do you want to lead the market or react to the market?" If you have invested the time and effort to initially build the "e" competence, be a leader.

In this chapter, we will review the basics of *housekeeping*. Once a business has been enabled, business risks have changed and should be assessed. The risk assessment will focus on four main areas:

1. *Security:* As you establish each Web application, you increase business risk to unauthorized users. Good housekeeping requires periodic review of security.
2. *Performance:* Each application will perform a specific function and should be monitored using consistent metrics and should also be monitored for possible enhancements.
3. *Appearance:* If you intend to project a well-managed business, you will want to be sure that the Web applications appear professional and up to date.
4. *Training:* Now that you have designed your website purpose, you will want to understand the skills necessary to navigate your website. Consider the intended audience and be sure that there is enough information for users to accomplish the desired goals.

It is important that an enabled company project its technical and business competence through its website. A *current* website (e.g., updated daily with events and press releases) will demonstrate a high degree of professionalism to your constituents. What was your impression of a website with outdated material on the site, such as a promotion that expired 2 weeks prior?

You will also want to be sure that software upgrades are timely and represent current technology (use PayPal, credit cards, affinity marketing programs, and so on) and are properly installed. The source of information for these upgrades will be your software vendors and all e-business team members.

Last, you will want anyone who will be using the website to use it properly. Recurrent training, even if brief and on the website, may be important to your users. If you are going to remain competitive, you will want to periodically refresh your site to reflect changes in competitive conditions and software application enhancements.

Business Risk Assessment

Enablement requires that you change business processes and potentially expose your systems to unauthorized use. Applications open to the public have varying degrees of business risk that must be evaluated. Clearly, if you change the images on your website, there is little serious risk either immediately or in the future. However, if you were to add Web order processing, business risk would change considerably. The key to the risk assessment is to catalog all the enablement changes made and analyze the potential ancillary implications resulting from Web enablement. An activity as simple as e-mail makes the company vulnerable to viruses and worms, so be thorough in your assessment.

Use a master checklist of the all the website changes, grouped in a meaningful way, such as by function (e.g., sales, research and development [R&D]) or by activity for the company (e.g., order processing, cash payments) within the matrix. Exhibit 10.1 shows a listing of the functions and the changes made to a company. The *listing includes all functions,* regardless of changes made within the functional area because a *master list will force the reviewer to consider all aspects of enablement.* In this checklist, the reviewer will document all the processes that have been affected by the enablement. Many different processes could be affected by the enablement, and each requires a risk assessment. In this particular example, although product master files may be affected by online processing, mitigating controls over these subsystems minimizes the risk. However, sales commissions are considered high risk because we may directly impact sales compensation.

Exhibit 10.1

Risk Analysis

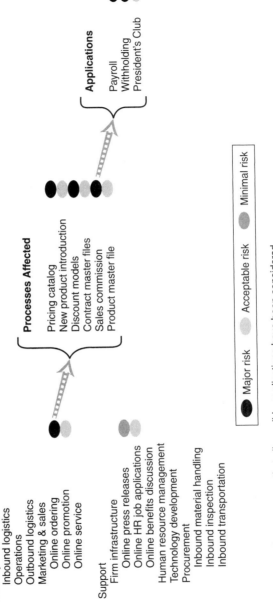

Function

Primary
 Inbound logistics
 Operations
 Outbound logistics
 Marketing & sales
  Online ordering
  Online promotion
  Online service

Support
 Firm infrastructure
  Online press releases
  Online HR job applications
  Online benefits discussion
 Human resource management
 Technology development
 Procurement
  Inbound material handling
  Inbound inspection
  Inbound transportation

Processes Affected

Pricing catalog
New product introduction
Discount models
Contract master files
Sales commission
Product master file

Applications

Payroll
Withholding
President's Club

● Major risk   ● Acceptable risk   ● Minimal risk

1. List all functions to ensure that all possible applications have been considered.
2. Assess business risk.
3. Identify all applications that are affected by the changes.
4. Assess business risk.
5. Identify Web applications and hardware affected by the changes.
6. Assess business risk.

The checklists in Exhibit 10.1 should be used within the company for all major business segments, whether centralized or decentralized; remote sites with self-contained applications should be evaluated separately. It is important to ensure that all areas affected by the enablement be considered because of the exposure to unauthorized use or tampering, financial, or market risk to the company.

Security

Security is critical as you enable your company because you are exposing the company to unauthorized users who can take information from your site (e.g., customer lists, employee lists), hackers who can modify your site or process unauthorized transactions, or well-intentioned authorized users who can improperly use the site, destroy data, or disrupt processing. To maintain control and avoid problems, only qualified and properly authorized personnel should install, modify, and activate features on the website. Today, viruses/worms and hackers continually develop new methods to hack computer systems, where even the most secure organizations have been hacked (e.g., Bank of America). Creative and malicious people develop worms and viruses that disable, disrupt, or alter websites or download confidential and secure data. Security and business risk should be analyzed, and effective hardware and software solutions to security risks must be implemented and maintained.

Once installed, the security measures should be properly maintained, and all users should be especially vigilant to unauthorized access and downloads. Software and hardware vendors routinely issue alerts, software patches, and updated software based on their investigation of Web activity. All companies that have been enabled should maintain close working relationships with the software and hardware vendors to ensure that they receive alerts and software/hardware enhancements.

If you have not enabled your company, security risk still increases if anyone in your company accesses the Web for research or communication with any outside organization. Be sure that you install and maintain adequate security measures to avoid catastrophic systems problems.

Security also includes privacy for all the information included on the website. Although the company may not suffer any direct loss as a result of being hacked, you do not want the negative publicity of failed security and a compromised website. Recall that in early 2004, the credit card processing company responsible for processing Wal-Mart transactions was hacked and lost several thousand confidential files. Security must also protect information that is not necessarily company proprietary.

Performance

Web performance will be visible to all who use the system. Baseline metrics should be established and monitored to ensure that the website is useful. Response time, "clicks-to-order," percentage of discontinued transactions, uptime, peak transaction periods, types of transactions, source of transactions, return users, and so forth, can be compared against historical trends, industry averages, and best in class. Each of these comparisons represents an opportunity to improve your competitiveness.

Effective housekeeping requires that once you initialize the system, you begin tracking the metrics that are most important and summarize and report on the performance periodically. Industry and global metrics are often available to monitor your competitiveness.

Appearance

An enabled organization will continuously review the technical and esoteric elements of the Web. Each element of your Web enablement should be monitored to ensure that the company's sites are up to date and present the company as a modern, competitive organization. What was your impression of a website that displayed an expired promotion or in July displayed the *spring line of clothes*. Appearance can be as simple as type sizes and site navigation actions or as complex as streaming video with real-time interaction or integrated telecommunications features. Whatever the role of the website, be sure that the appearance represents the company effectively.

Appearance also includes the time to interact and download information. If your website displays streaming video, loading pages may be too slow and the user may become impatient and leave before you have accomplished your goal. Although security is important, if systems' settings are too conservative, interaction may be too limited—for example, antivirus software deletes file attachments, e-mails are rejected for forbidden yet innocent words, and so forth. Appearance requires judgment to be sure standards are reasonable.

Training

Once you have invested the resources to enable your company and secure your sites, be sure that you train both the current and expected users. This is difficult because Web applications will be designed for primary users—perhaps the most frequent users, or most valuable users to the company—but should also anticipate other users that may be worthwhile to the company.

Also, the target user may change as Web usage increases. If the site is too simple, it may be cumbersome to experienced users. Too many graphics may slow access for dial-up applications, but too few will make the site unattractive.

As you continually upgrade—perhaps on standard Web life cycles or as available from software and hardware vendors—you want to be sure that your target users are able to effectively use the site. Online notification of changes, and perhaps online training for unique features, would be useful for your constituents. Also, anyone who interacts with site users should be well trained to be sure that the *real-time* medium does not bog down with information delays or misinformation.

The Process

Exhibit 10.2 is a summary of a housekeeping planning worksheet. The basis of the worksheet is a complete inventory of hardware, software, and content included in any Web application. Each component should be reviewed periodically to ensure that the basic elements of good housekeeping are achieved—security, performance, appearance, and training. Individuals are responsible for the review and will establish appropriate review cycles.

Examples of some routine housekeeping activities that you should have in your plans include the following:

- *Cycle refreshment* should include content, application software, and hardware. This may be difficult because the Internet pace is rapid and unpredictable. Establish a minimum refreshment cycle (e.g., review the content at least weekly) but also provide for those unpredictable changes in the website to present information that is current. Current application software and hardware depend on vendor updates and should be monitored by the respective people in the organization. This should include the information technology function, but all users should continually observe vendor releases and competitive and other websites to be sure that you are current. Cycle refreshment will also include responses to queries and observations from the *contact us* or *frequently asked questions* section of any well-designed website. Be sure that you have defined responsibilities for all such contacts, including response times. What value is a real-time website if it requires 2 weeks to get a qualified response? Actively manage the cycle times.

Exhibit 10.2

Housekeeping—Planning

	Responsibility	Daily	Weekly	Monthly	Quarterly	Annually
Hardware Systems						
Various						
Content						
Functional						
Departments						
Marketing	Dir. Marketing				✓	
Security	Dir. IT					✓
Performance	Dir. Marketing			✓		
Appearance	Dir. Marketing				✓	
Training	Mgr. Marketing					
Regulatory	Dir. Reg. Affairs				✓	
Consumer						
Awareness	Dir. Consumer Affairs			✓	✓	
Security	Dir. IT			✓		
Performance	Dir. Consumer Affairs		✓			
Appearance	Dir. Consumer Affairs				✓	
Training	Dir. Consumer Affairs				✓	
Consumer						
Complaints	VP Marketing	✓		✓	✓	✓
Software Systems						
Various						

Notes:
- Review frequency depends on company impact.
- Consumer feedback through the Web should be handled daily—establish a required response time metric.
- Monthly and quarterly may include a review of the site, but also statistical analysis, response times, click-through analysis, and so forth.
- A specific person is responsible for performance so that accountability is direct and measurable.

- *Competitive websites, industry websites, and the entire Web* should be reviewed on a minimum cycle to be sure that the company is up to date. Establish the review cycle based on the risks and opportunities in your industry and applications already implemented. You will always want to be state of the art in critical activities such as order processing, cash applications, product and service technical bulletins, and so forth.
- *Functionality and application upgrades* and new functions and applications should be scheduled so that the appearance is one of continuous improvement. You do not have to upgrade everything simultaneously, but the constituents will have a more positive image of your company if you periodically improve functionality. In nearly any company, there is a long list of functions, applications, and Web improvement that can be implemented. List and prioritize the applications based on the benefits and costs to the company, and schedule periodic functionality improvements. The frequency will depend on the company's competitive position, the industry, and the company strategy. Although there is no *best* timing, be assured that annually is not satisfactory.

Exhibit 10.3 displays the various levels that may be considered in the housekeeping chores to properly maintain a website. The exhibit displays a matrix that includes cycle frequency as well as the key elements of the review (security, performance, appearance, and training) for all the functional areas. This could be further expanded to include the various activities within the functions (e.g., cash payments, ordering, shipping). The key to effective housekeeping is to anticipate problems and build a review cycle that minimizes business risk.

Exhibit 10.3 includes a column for responsibility, which must be specific to ensure complete accountability. Ambiguity will lead to loss of control.

Summary

Web enablement is a simple process that requires well-thought-out plans, assessment of the environment, and a clear understanding of the business objectives and the competitive environment. It takes time and energy to establish a properly functioning, fully enabled company, but it is worth the effort. Lead—do not follow—to improve your competitive position, and you will succeed, because as leaders, you will engage all the employees, customers, and vendors—basically all the constituents—that are affected by your business.

Exhibit 10.3

Housekeeping—Number of Dimensions

	Responsibility	Daily	Weekly	Monthly	Quarterly	Annually
Hardware Systems						
Servers		✓			✓	✓
Communications					✓	
BlackBerry	IT			✓		
Cellular	Telecom			✓		
Wireless	Telecom			✓		
VOIP	IT			✓		
Conference video	IT			✓		
Remote access	IT			✓	✓	
Laptops				✓		✓
Wireless	IT			✓	✓	
Conference video	IT					
Training	IT			✓	✓	✓
Software Systems						
VOIP	IT			✓		✓
Conferencing	IT				✓	
Security						
Software upgrades	IT	✓		✓	✓	✓
Failures/follow-up	IT	✓	✓	✓	✓	✓
Training	IT			✓	✓	✓
Content						
Functional departments						
Marketing	Marketing	✓	✓			
Regulatory	Reg			✓	✓	
Consumer awareness	Consumer Affairs			✓	✓	
Finance	Finance			✓	✓	
Legal	Legal			✓	✓	
Sales—Web	Sales Operations	✓	✓	✓		
Sales—Web	Sales Mgmt.				✓	✓
Frequently asked questions	All	✓				
Consumer complaints	Consumer Affairs	✓		✓	✓	✓
Web pages						
Home	All			✓		
Financial information	Finance			✓	✓	✓
Product help function	Prod. Development			✓		
Other sites— cross-reference						
Department of Labor	HR			✓		
Department of Health, Education, and Welfare	HR		✓			
Training	All			✓	✓	✓

E-business is not a technology but a mind-set that will ensure your continued competitiveness. Through continuous improvement, monitoring of the applications and hardware, open communication channels, and hard work, you will have the most competitive website in your industry—because you have prepared a process that will ensure you are aware of improvements in your industry and all other sites.

CHAPTER 11

WHERE DO WE GO FROM HERE?

Introduction

Throughout this book, we have reviewed activities and strategies that will help us redirect our company resources using the Web to be more effective in the competitive global economy. Business rules have changed, and the environment has become more volatile and competitive compared with a decade ago. In the past, we knew our competitors and customers. Globalization has changed that familiarity, and executives are often uncomfortable as a result. Executives can view the new environment either as a threat or an opportunity, or they can attempt to ignore the change entirely. This book outlines steps that will allow you to lead the competition in the new global environment, but the transition will not be easy. Traditional business timetables will accelerate, and the changes in our organization need to be prioritized and actively managed.

E-business is not a technology, but a way of thinking and a tool to make our business more competitive. Soon e-business will be pervasive in every company and organization, and we must decide whether we will lead or follow in the next few years.

As "C"-level executives, we are hired to improve our company performance. Typical metrics that measure improved performance include higher sales, a faster rate of new product introductions, improved gross profit, and lower expense-to-sales ratios. These and most other performance measures will be improved using e-business methods without entirely reconstructing our business. When accumulated, the numerous small incremental changes possible with the Web individually add minimal value to our business performance, but overall they will yield impressive results. Exhibit 11.1 reflects how small incremental changes to costs can dramatically improve earnings. Note that less than a 10 percent change in resource will lead to nearly a 50 percent increase in earnings.

Culture change, and not technology, drives an e-business to adapt to the rapidly and ever-changing business environment. If 20 existing or new competitors increase market share by only 0.5 percent, they will take 10 percent from someone. If we *improve communications, research capabilities, and transaction*

Exhibit 11.1

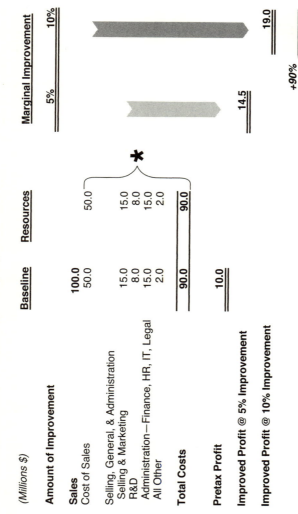

Average Company Profit and Loss

(Millions $)

	Baseline	Resources
Amount of Improvement		
Sales	**100.0**	
Cost of Sales	50.0	50.0
Selling, General, & Administration		
Selling & Marketing	15.0	15.0
R&D	8.0	8.0
Administration—Finance, HR, IT, Legal	15.0	15.0
All Other	2.0	2.0
Total Costs	**90.0**	**90.0**
Pretax Profit	**10.0**	

Improved Profit @ 5% Improvement

Improved Profit @ 10% Improvement

Marginal Improvement

5%	10%
14.5	19.0

+45%   +90%

Marginal improvements add up to big profit increases.

206

processing using e-business, we gain the market share. Let's look at some examples:

- *Improved sales:* Initially, we may think of direct selling over the Web as the best method to use e-business, but e-business will also expand sales through improved new product development (e.g., research and development [R&D] using global resources), new ventures that would previously be impractical, potential information and data sales (e.g., selling information that is resident in company data systems), and/or extended service programs that are now possible using Web communication.
- *Expense improvement:* It is not just expense reduction that can be achieved using the Web. Once expenses are analyzed (e.g., by function, activity, and direct/indirect categories), use the Web to improve the value achieved—for example, shift from indirect to direct categories to improve customer relationships. If the expense has minimal benefit, eliminate it altogether. As you identify expenses that generate minimal value, shift the spending to areas that will improve performance and relationships and expand the business.
- *Reduced capital:* E-business will reduce the capital required to run the business. The Web is instant and creates shorter business cycle times throughout the entire value chain. Reduced working capital investments (e.g., inventory, accounts receivable) and fixed assets are possible when the Web is used effectively.

Why E-Business? Increase Company Value

E-business companies have higher price-earnings (P-E) multiples, not just because they are more profitable today than their peers but also because they are progressive and likely to create more future wealth. The companies have access to broader geographic markets, higher-value product lines, and overall better results from fewer resources because their employees are trained to deliver *more for less, and faster.*

GE, Dell, eBay, and Amazon.com are considered leaders and are some of the most progressive companies in the world. These companies have integrated e-business technology into their value chain and developed new methods for doing business. They dominate their industries, some of which did not even exist a decade ago. The leadership teams at Web-enabled companies thoroughly understand their business and their impact on company performance:

- *Functions:* The executives know their value chain and have selectively adapted technology to the most important functions. They do not attempt to enable every function immediately.
- *Activities:* The executives analyze their company's activities, eliminate the non- or low-value-added activities, shift resources from indirect activities to direct activities, and whenever possible, use technology to improve the processes.
- *Constituents:* Executives know their constituents and constantly seek ways to improve company performance. The executives do not limit themselves to considering only today's constituents; they include potential constituents as well—those beyond the horizon.

Study an *enabled* company (Dell, GE, Amazon.com, or eBay) to understand how well they execute functional activities, how they manage existing relationships, and how they develop new constituents. It is inevitable that highly competitive companies will adopt e-business tools to beat the competition, so why would we not adapt sooner rather than later?

Critical Success Factors in E-Business

Hundreds of factors affect a successful e-business conversion; several of the most significant are discussed in the following sections.

Leadership and Teams Are Critical

"C"-level leadership is essential. We must evaluate the business, define priorities, and actively manage the conversion process, which is largely a culture change. Make e-business a high priority, manage using periodic progress reports, and link personal compensation to e-business performance for the best results. Make key managers part of the solution by involving them in analysis, goal-setting, and leadership roles within the company. When the culture is right, the entire organization will continuously seek business improvements by monitoring competitors and other businesses. Make e-business part of every employee's job responsibility. As leaders, be responsible for understanding enablement benefits; the rewards will occur over many years rather than just a short term.

Involve the Entire Organization

Being an enabled company means that we have delegated responsibility and authority throughout the organization. Do not be alarmed by what appears to be an environment outside our control, because if the company is supported by an organization of constituents—employees, agents, customers, vendors, and government agencies—our competitiveness will improve. We do not need extensive research departments to identify the trend because our constituents keep us informed—if we listen. Open the communication path, seek unbiased input, and let the organization analyze and present the information.

Public Goals

Keep the company's goals open and public so that team members not only feel responsible for performance but also enjoy a sense of accomplishment as goals are achieved. This will also encourage teamwork behind the scenes.

Time and Sense of Urgency Are Critical

Speed differentiates an enabled company from others, so accelerate the business pace and increase the sense of urgency. We will need self-discipline in the executive ranks to accelerate the pace and keep up with our constituents and the competition.

Analyze the Value Chain

Analyze our value chain and do not get bogged down in extensive detail—prioritize the review to the most likely areas for improvement. Include operations executives, and use their experience and knowledge to analyze the company and identify preliminary improvement projects. Prioritize the opportunities based on value added and not just expense reductions. Value-added measures may include new product sales, expanded geographic sales, new trade channels, product line extensions (e.g., adding a level of service to the sale to improve profits), reduced working capital requirements (e.g., lower inventories, receivables), lower fixed asset investments, or reduced expense levels.

Brainstorm e-business alternatives with the executive team, and engage outside experts to further develop strategies and plans if appropriate. As plans are developed, rank the *size, timing,* and *probability of success* of each venture to be sure that we have measurable accountability and checkpoints for the ventures. Include names and dates on plans to avoid wasting resources on unplanned and less valuable alternatives. As we review investment alternatives, do not become enamored with a particular technology. Execute only those plans that create value.

Adapt the Company to the New Economy

E-business will become more important during the next 5 years because the opportunities for global competitors will only increase. India and China were hidden treasures with underdeveloped infrastructures and no easy way to access their talent pools. Today, the Web has given access to these markets and others that were inaccessible only 10 years ago. The macro affects of the Web have altered the competitive landscape. Exhibit 11.2 shows how each of the five factors can impact virtually any business.

- *Pace:* Activities occur at a faster pace than in the past. Mail can now move at the speed of light (e-mail on optical fiber) rather than be constrained by physical movement, and e-mail is a richer medium with no activity fee. Personal and business communication today that is not completed by phone or in person is done through e-mail. This benefits the organization originating the transactions (less administrative cost and no postage or stationary) and allows a much richer communication (including hotlinks, full motion video, color images, and so on). In addition, the recipient can be anywhere in the world with Web access to retrieve and respond to the mail instantly.
- *Architecture:* Once we accelerate the business pace and are exposed to the world, how do we manage the flow of information? If we keep the same policies and processes that have survived for decades, can we remain competitive? As a business or individual, we can no longer control access to our e-mail account that may be prominently listed on our website, business card, and stationary, and we cannot control message boards and blogs displayed on the Web. Change the company architecture, policy, and procedures to deal with the openness and comparatively unrestrained access to information. Manage the environment rather than control every activity.
- *Globalization:* This is not just the globe and all the countries that we now have access to and which have access to us, but globalization could be limited to the United States but well beyond current self-imposed borders. Using the Web, small companies can now appear to be large, and larger companies can now perform in a much more

Exhibit 11.2

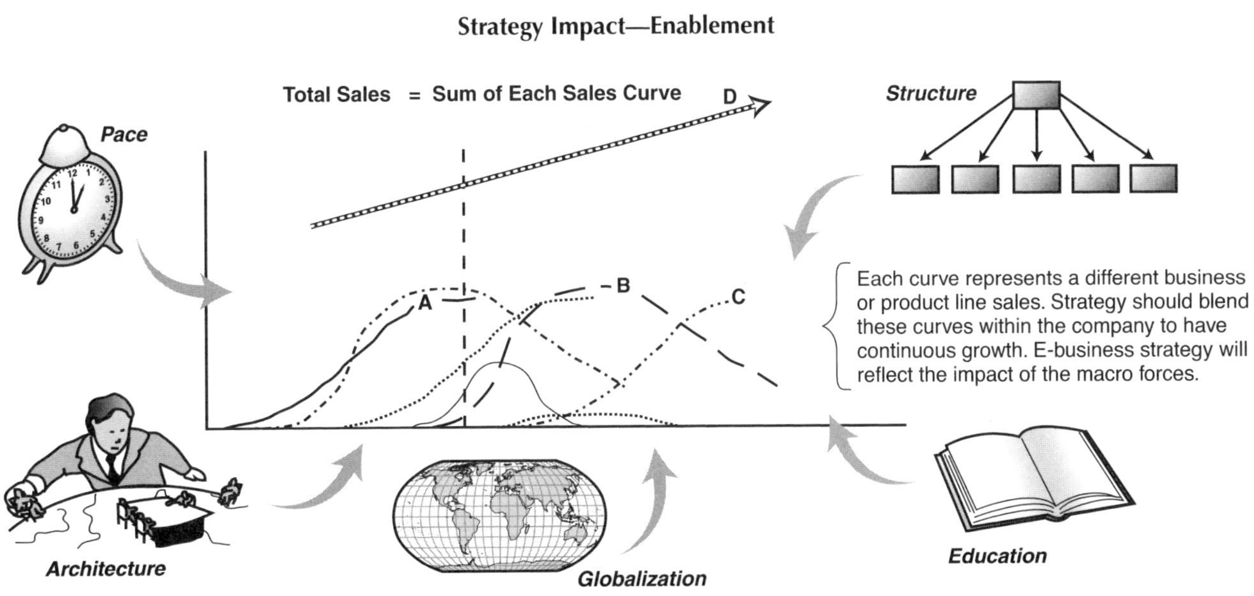

Strategy Impact—Enablement

Total Sales = Sum of Each Sales Curve

Structure

Each curve represents a different business or product line sales. Strategy should blend these curves within the company to have continuous growth. E-business strategy will reflect the impact of the macro forces.

A

B

C

D

Pace

Globalization

Education

Architecture

Each product has a different life cycle affected by the five macro e-business factors. An effective e-business strategy will embrace each of these factors and accelerate the business processes to improve the business value.

personal or local manner. Adapt to globalization to excel in the marketplace.

- *Education:* This is not Web technology training but rather educating our constituents to adapt to a Web-enabled business. Think about the cultural changes needed to deal with the expanded business opportunities—not just selling to those international locations but also buying products, sharing research, and developing legal relationships with them. How will our employees, contract agents, affiliates, and joint ventures deal with the new reality? Identify these education gaps and train the constituents to be successful.

- *Structure:* If the business pace accelerates and operations extend globally, how will our current constituents deal with the changes? Examine the organization structure, identify areas that will not function effectively in the new environment, and modify the structure to improve performance.

When we use the Web, *improvements need not be all or nothing.* Use small steps and pilot projects to limit risk and build competence and confidence. Because the environment changes frequently, we will never be left too far behind the competition if we continuously improve.

Competitors Will Change . . . Can We Stay the Same?

In a Web-enabled world, we cannot easily predict the competitive environment. Andy Grove, in his book *Only the Paranoid Survive: How to Exploit the Crisis Points That Challenge Every Company,* recognized that the business environment has irrevocably changed to one that is a more democratic process—one with few rules of competition, except that things will change and the pace will accelerate. Executives cannot exclusively examine existing competitive products, competitors, current suppliers, and customers to formulate future strategies. Today, executives must look beyond the traditional horizon because the pace is faster and the rigid rules do not exist. "This is the time when relying on the past or on conventional wisdom can lead you rapidly to disaster. The old ways don't work in this age of lightning-fast change, high volatility, global hypercompetition, declining prices, and compressed margins. New threats and opportunities arise faster and more often. The next assault on your ability to make money can come from almost anywhere. You have to study your extended industry, which includes all the players who influence the industry's behaviors and economics. Increasingly, they can upend your old assumptions. Who, ten years earlier, would have predicted that Wal-Mart in 2003 would be one of America's biggest sellers of groceries, books and music?"[46]

Housekeeping Discipline Is Essential

Do not believe that once we upgrade processes, and so on, to be Web enabled that the job is done. Recall how fast our new global economy moves. In less than a decade, the North American Free Trade Agreement (NAFTA) has become nearly irrelevant, as India and China have become global suppliers and consumers. What is competitive today will become outdated in a much shorter cycle time than 5 years ago. Do not allow your website, Web procedures, and organization to become stale. If you do not maintain, refresh, and expand enablement processes, your company will fall behind the competitors.

If we manage the housekeeping process correctly, we will have two sources for input: the competition and the constituents that we have empowered to keep us current. If our company has 1,000 employees, why not engage each of those 1,000 employees to be our advocates to remain competitive? Our constituents also include customers (build a relationship using the Web) and suppliers (expand the relationship to encourage their creative solutions that will improve value for them and us—it is not a zero sum venture). If we energize the e-business leaders in our organization, and they in turn energize their staffs, our advocacy will be multiplied. But this requires work—it is not a simple task.

Summary

We are responsible for the success of our company. The tools are readily available for us to lead the company into the future in a very competitive manner. To be effective, we must embrace the *enabled* strategy and use the tools to remain ahead of the competition. If we are behind the competition, remember that business cycle times have accelerated and the cycle time also means that a quick recovery is possible.

It's up to you.

---

[46] "Confronting Reality," by staff writer, *Fortune Magazine,* October 18, 2004, pp. 225–231.

INDEX

Note: Page numbers in *italics* indicate exhibits.

About TEXERE

Texere, a progressive and authoritative voice in business publishing, brings to the global business community the expertise and insights of leading thinkers. Our books educate, enlighten, and entertain, and provide an intersection where our authors and our readers share cutting edge ideas, practices, and innovative solutions. Texere seeks to cultivate, enhance, and disseminate information that illuminates the global business landscape.

www.thomson.com/learning/texere

About the typeface

This book was set in 10.5/14 pt Bembo. Bembo was cut by Francesco Griffo for the Venitian printer Aldus Manutius to publish in 1495 *De Aetna* by Cardinal Pietro Bembo. Stanley Morison supervised the design of Bembo for the Monotype Corporation in 1929. The Bembo is a readable and classical typeface because of its well-proportioned letterforms, functional serifs, and lack of peculiarities.

Library of Congress Cataloging-in-Publication Data

Gendron, Michael.
   Creating the new e-business company : innovative strategies for real-world applications / Michael P. Gendron.
      p. cm.
   ISBN 0-324-22485-0
   1. Electronic commerce—Management. 2. Technological innovations—Management. 3. Information technology—Management. 4. Industrial management. I. Title.
   HF5548.32.G45 2006
   658.8'72—dc22

                                                        2005023671